AFRICAN ELEPHANTS

AFRICAN

Reinhard Künkel

ELEPHANTS

Harry N. Abrams, Inc., Publishers

African Elephants is a substantially revised edition of *Elephants*, published by Harry N. Abrams, Inc., in 1982.

Library of Congress Catalog Card Number: 98-73803
ISBN 0-8109-1984-2

First published in Great Britain in 1998 by The Harvill Press

Designed by Derek Birdsall

Printed and bound in Italy

Harry N. Abrams, Inc.
100 Fifth Avenue
New York, N.Y. 10011
www.abramsbooks.com

Contents

Acknowledgements

To Lala, with whom I love to share life and wildlife

This book is also dedicated to the memory of two friends,
Eckart Müller and Maleko, who lived continents apart
but shared the wonderful ability to inspire the people
around them with their warmth and humour

I have just read through the acknowledgements to the first edition of this book. They mention the help and support I received from many people in Tanzania while working on *Elephants*. Since it was published I have taken part in many other projects, including a film on elephants, in the course of which I received still more help and advice. So here is an excellent opportunity to thank all those people who have, over many years, supported my work in Tanzania's wonderful national parks and game reserves, true heritage sites of Africa and of all humankind.

The cradle of mankind might have been left by its first inhabitants, the early hominids, but the knowledge that this spectacular landscape has hardly changed since mankind took its first steps gives me an extra thrill when I try to portray the same wildlife that the people who left their footprints at Laetoli some 3.6 million years ago might have known. I have been a guest in this country for a long time and over the years many people have given me that precious feeling of being welcome. And I still appreciate every day of my life amongst the wildlife. My sincere thanks go to the Tanzanian government and its officials, who so generously allowed me to wander with my cameras and mind through this ancient part of their land, filled as it is with the most beautiful wildlife in the world.

I owe thanks to far more people than I can mention. I am thinking of those who pushed me out of mud holes, treated me to a warm cup of tea or just gave me a passing smile on the road. I remember the little herdsboy who one day joined me for an otherwise lonely lunch. Armed only with a spear and a young heart full of courage, he shepherded his animals across the endless plains. We had no common language, but sharing the land and the sky for a moment made us friends. He helped me to understand.

I will not again list the people I thanked by name in the first edition of this book. Too much time has passed. Some have left this world, others have moved on. But I still remember them gratefully and I hope to thank them all with the scenes and reflections of their elephants printed in this book.

I want to mention the names of a few people without whose support my new elephant work could not have happened, especially Mr E. Chausi, the conservator of the Ngorongoro Conservation Area, who so warmly welcomed us back to this splendid Garden of Eden, as many visitors call the Ngorongoro Crater, after my wife and I had explored life and wildlife on the Australian continent for a year. It had been great fun and we were very tempted to stay. The people of Ngorongoro and other friends helped us to decide to continue working in Tanzania.

In this context I would like to thank Dr Richard Faust, president, and Dr Markus Borner, regional director, of the Frankfurt Zoological Society, who supported us in many ways. Both men are strongly committed to continuing the pioneering conservation work Professor Berhard Grzimek started decades ago, the essence of which is contained in his famous appeal: "Serengeti shall not die."

Aadje Geertsema and Margaret and Per Kullander invited us to stay at their Ndutu Safari Lodge on the Serengeti plains. It is a fabulous home from which to explore the surrounding plains and woodlands, the heart of the annual wildebeest migration during the rainy season. Sometimes the elephants move right through nature's endless garden spreading in front of our windows, to our everlasting joy. Thanks to our generous friends.

The people of the Ndutu Safari Lodge not only treat their guests to a special atmosphere, but also keep our cars together (not an easy task!), feed us (Little John's pancakes are the best in the world) and help us with the hundreds of problems everyday life in the bush offers one as challenge. And it is all done with a smile. Thanks to Leonard and Moody, to Little John and Ndelay, Marcelli and Josef, Hamisi and Mirando, Bifa and Augustin — I certainly would love to name them all, but then there would not be enough pages left for the elephants, so these few names have to stand for the great team of Ndutu. Thank you very much.

And thanks to Leonce and Mohamed too, and to Paul and Louise, who joined as managers just in time for the special challenges of a long El Niño season. I think few of the many people who come through on safari realize what an enormous amount of organisation it takes to run a lodge in the middle of nowhere. It is more than a full-time job and requires all the energy, competence and imagination that can be mustered. And still, sometimes humour is all that is left to keep the links together. Aadje and Margaret, we appreciate your work! It allows us to forget about logistics and face our own specific set of problems. Like finding the elephants. They are big animals. But the forest is even bigger. Whole herds can disappear into the woodlands along the Olduvai Gorge. And do. It is wonderful to be free to look at them. Again our thanks.

Barbie Allen, as always, supported my work and this book, with her inspiring advice, strength and humour, not to mention providing a vital communication link and a home in the last stage of the production of this book. Many thanks.

Reinhard "Leo" Künkel
Ndutu Safari Lodge
Ngorongoro Conservation Area
Tanzania
June 1998

Preface

Elephants are the biggest animals walking this planet. They are unique and fascinating creatures, inspiring us with awe, curiosity and joy. With calm and dignity they have wandered through the depths of evolutionary time. Only during the last tenth of that time have they had to share their land with our early ancestors.

When the human population explosion took off, elephant time and human time began to split. Elephants continued their endless wanderings. They barely changed. We did. It was unnoticeable at first. Only in the last few seconds of geological time did these changes gain an ever-increasing momentum, with disastrous results for elephants. Already extinct in many areas of their former range, their time is now running out fast.

A few months ago I visited some friends on their farm. They have a little three-year-old daughter. While we were busy putting new life into the old evergreen of farmers' talk, I noticed that she was watching me with great intensity. A few minutes later I glanced at her again. Her gaze was still focused on me. Suddenly she pointed a tiny finger at my chest. Only then did I realise that it was not me, but the elephant adorning my sweater, that had caught her eye. While I told her of those enormous but gentle giants living in a far-off land, her eyes grew bigger and bigger. She was spellbound.

We must hope that humankind finds the generosity and strength to save the few small islands of elephant land that were created this century in the form of national parks and game reserves. It will not be easy. The shock waves of that silent explosion have already reached these shores and are pushing against them with growing force.

The sketches and scenes reflected in the following pages are an attempt to freeze some of the moments of that precious time. Without elephants and the extraordinary wildlife living in their shade, life on earth would be infinitely poorer. And our children, in the centuries to come, would never forgive us if one day there were no elephants left for them to love.

African Morning

The rising sun hovered above a dead tree, its blaze seeming to singe the wing-tips of two crested cranes who were late in leaving their sleeping place. On the lake, pelicans fluttered clumsily to their fishing grounds. Some impalas strolled along the shore. Reflected in the shimmering water, their slender shapes lost all colour and weight and became graceful silhouettes stalking through liquid silver. A hippopotamus bull emerged from the bushes. Announcing his coming with one high- and five low-pitched trumpet blasts, he lumbered across the sand, splashed into the water, and disappeared into a group of dark hippopotamus backs that rose from the waves a hundred yards offshore. The hippos would spend the day dozing in the water; only at dark would they return to land to graze.

I sat on the roof of my Land Rover enjoying the cool air and soft light, letting my field glasses sweep across the African landscape. The steep sides of the rift valley rise, in places, 2600 feet above Lake Manyara, and to these heights the elephants had climbed during the night. Soon I picked out one group wandering along a winding ridge; a little below, a second group was descending a steep path. The clear morning promised a hot day, and the elephants were leaving their nocturnal pastures early enough to reach the acacia forests and watering places before the heat grew too intense. On cool, rainy days, by contrast, it might be noon before they returned to the plain. Their swaying movements, trunks swinging like pendulums, kept them in balance on the precipitous terrain. Their heads bobbed to the rhythm of their steps, making their ears flap around their shoulders like the sails of becalmed ships. Despite the difficult and dangerous descent, the animals seemed completely relaxed, often stopping to pluck grass and leaves. A young bull playfully snatched a long branch and chewed on its tip. Only one cow with a calf in tow was restless and aggressive. With a violent swing of her tusks, she shoved aside an adolescent bull who had probably come too close; he briefly lost his footing and slipped a few yards downhill.

The elephants roamed the steep slopes like colossal mountain goats, repeatedly interrupting their descent to eat at length. They plucked bushes to shreds, dug for roots and broke large branches from the few trees that had taken root at those heights. On reaching gentler slopes, they halted briefly under a baobab, perhaps to rest or to reconnoitre the land below — then abruptly took off again at a lively pace, as if in sudden haste to reach the acacia forests, which finally swallowed them up in a jumble of trunks, branches, fallen trees and shifting shadow and light.

A few hours later, sitting under a tree, I witnessed an arresting spectacle: a herd of about eighty elephants passing in a broad front through the acacia grove. The wind was favourable so that the elephants could not pick up my scent. They approached, grew larger, became gigantic, and finally were so close that I could hear the sand crunch under their soft, flat feet. One contingent slipped past my hiding place at a distance of barely twenty yards. The silence of their drifting passage was astounding until they came to a deeply cut riverbed that lay across the path to their watering place. There, two of the calves immediately collapsed into the sand and slid down on their bellies. They burrowed their trunks playfully into the soft ground and spewed trunkloads of dust on each other's backs. They then ran exuberantly through the dry bed, each step powdering the air with a jet of sand. The herd had almost disappeared into the brush on the opposite bank before these two abandoned their game and hurried to join their elders, who were placidly swaying through the bush.

Flight

I was driving along a bumpy track that led down to the river. The valley lay in shadow, apparently empty, and tree trunks and underbrush blocked my view. I drove around a bend and there, suddenly, were elephants – only a few, but all very large. As startled as I was, I brought the car to a skidding, squealing, dust-billowing halt, but the elephants were not mollified. Angry trumpet signals shrilled through the thicket, accompanied by energetic flapping of ears and indignant shaking of heads. The underbrush splintered under the stomping. I withdrew as fast as I could, for my own safety but also because I hoped by retreating to restore their tranquillity.

But there was no quieting them. My abrupt and unexpected arrival had plunged them into panic. From a small elevation that offered a view of the valley I discovered that the fellows I had disturbed were but the small advance guard of a struggling herd totalling about one hundred, among which the panic began to spread like brushfire. Their trumpeting, at once frightened and furious, swelled to an apocalyptic chorus that shattered the forlorn stillness of the morning. A hundred elephants roared through the valley. Branches snapped, saplings toppled, impenetrable undergrowth was trampled flat. A cloud of dust rose into the air like an ominous distress signal – a fog that enveloped the herd in ghostly light. At moments, I could distinguish the shape of a calf among the racing giants, anxiously trying to keep up with its mother.

The elephants kept running, fleeing headlong in blind terror, urging one another on with piercing cries of alarm. Half an hour after the spate of bodies, the grey dust and the strident din had finally been swallowed up around a river bend, I still heard occasional trumpet blasts in the far distance. Never had I seen elephants run so fast, so far.

At first, I had watched the stampede in a daze. Then I reproached myself for my awkwardness, which, I thought, had put the herd into headlong flight. But later, when I told the story to one of the gamekeepers, he had a different, more plausible explanation: elephants, being oblivious to the boundaries of their parks and preserves, sometimes wander through neighbouring territories, where angry farmers fearing for their crops fire warning shots to drive them away and where poachers shoot to kill. The herd I encountered may well have had some bitter experience not long before, which would account for their seemingly inordinate terror.

Valour and Discretion

On the plain by the lake was a spot where the ground lay bare. The elephants often came here to dig and eat the salt- and mineral-rich earth. They loosened the crusted soil with the hard toe-rims of their front feet, then shoved the lumps into their mouths with their trunks. Some cows, wanting more than they could loosen with their feet, went down on their knees to break up the earth with their tusks. Some of the younger animals also knelt down, trying to pick up the salt-rich substance directly with their mouths. The animals' craving for salt was obviously stronger even than mother love: the calves, trying continually to snatch some salt earth from their mothers, were invariably pushed aside.

The salt lick was much in demand; one group after another made for the shallow pit in the course of a morning. Since the salt lick could accommodate only one family unit at a time, impatient newcomers might attempt to drive the present occupants off. But a certain hierarchy among the lead cows seemed clearly to apply: if the approaching group was headed by a matriarch of higher rank, the current tenants would retreat at the first, often barely hinted threat. It follows that lower-ranking newcomers had to wait until their predecessors chose to leave.

Normally, the dissolved salt in the elephants' drinking water suffices to meet their need. They prefer water with a high concentration of minerals and sometimes undertake long treks to reach such watering places. In the absence of these, they will dig up the soil around natural salt licks; sometimes they even break up whole termite hills, which are as hard as concrete, simply to get at the enriched soil of these insect citadels. In the Ngorongoro Conservation Area there is a rock face with a cave deep enough and high enough comfortably to hold a fully grown, standing bull elephant. Tusk imprints reminiscent of chisel marks crisscross its walls and ceiling. These must have taken the elephants, in their search for salt, decades — if not centuries — to carve.

One morning I came upon an assembly of about eighty elephants in the vicinity of the salt lick, with five or six hundred buffalo grazing nearby. Two hours later, prompted by the growing heat, the elephants decamped for a mud bath to the only wallow of the region, closely followed by the buffalo. A silent phalanx of the latter surrounded the bathing elephants at a distance of about fifty yards. A few especially impatient buffalo bulls ventured closer, but about ten yards away they stopped in their tracks, stared motionlessly at the elephants for several minutes, suddenly shook their heads, and seconds later, resumed their transfixed staring.

After their mud bath, the elephants moved to the nearby salt lick. The buffalo followed in short order and surrounded them again. Gradually both herds streamed out onto the plain, the small groups of elephants looking like grey islands emerging from a sea of buffalo backs. The older elephants suffered the buffalos' impertinent proximity with equanimity, but an occasional juvenile tried to chase the intruders with threats and mock attacks. An enraged four- or five-year-old charged one buffalo who had ventured far too close, but when the offender did not budge and simply stared mistrustfully at his attacker, the young elephant, visibly chastened by such colossal fearlessness, hesitated briefly, then wheeled around and hurried back to the safety of his family. A more mature male, already endowed with arm-long tusks and a most impressive bulk, had better luck. His thrust, accompanied by irate trumpeting, drove his opponent back, if only ten or twenty yards.

Another time, I saw the lead cow of an elephant group rout an enormous buffalo from the wallow where he had dozed through the afternoon. On the whole, however, only young elephants will attack other animals, either in play or because they want to show off and are looking for a victim. I once observed a pubescent male stomping up and down a riverbed in seemingly violent rage, then, warrior and trumpeter in one, charge two wart-hogs whose only offence was to be digging for roots nearby. Tails pointing skywards, the hogs escaped.

In need of a new target, the young challenger then turned against six zebras grazing on the other side of the riverbed. Having frightened them into a brief canter, he crowned his efforts by scaring off some vultures that had been sitting on the bank, wings outstretched to dry after their morning ablutions. The rest of his troop ignored their impetuous comrade's exploits, browsing peacefully the while. Some days later, as the same elephants were passing a group of baboons, one of the calves suddenly veered, ears flapping, and rushed the startled primates, who escaped up the nearest tree, whence they railed at the troublemaker at the top of their voices. Impalas, who frequently browse near elephants, also become occasional targets of their adolescent exuberance, to which they generally respond with what seems appropriate nonchalance.

Despite their size, elephants by no means claim undisputed precedence in all their dealings with other animals. The privileges they might derive from their awesomeness and strength they are often too gentle and peaceable to claim. An elephant family, including an enormous bull, was resting by the edge of a pool, eyes shut, drowsing away the afternoon. Two crested cranes came stalking up in leisurely search of food. On reaching the water, they first quenched their thirst, then began prancing around each other with outspread wings. At the first steps of their mating dance the elephants rose abruptly and, to escape the annoying commotion, took off without a sound.

Normally, hippos spend daylight hours in the water, coming to shore to feed only at night. But one afternoon, on the plain by the Musasa River, a hippo strayed into a herd of elephants. One of the bulls headed menacingly for the myopic leviathan but lost heart after a few steps and beat a retreat, and the rest of the herd hurriedly opened a zigzag path for the waddling, agitated animal. When, very early the next morning, another hippo emerged from the thicket and headed slowly towards the river, browsing as he came, the feeding elephants gradually grew so disquieted at his approach that they crossed uneasily to the other bank.

An episode that unfolded in the Selous area illustrates even more clearly the mistrust of hippos that elephants display. Four elephants ambled along the shore of the Rufiji River where it fans out into several channels, finally finding a convenient ford. They slowly waded into the loamy current up to their bellies, then to their shoulders. A few more steps and the animals had to swim. Only the tops of their heads and their eyes protruded above the water, and the tips of their trunks poked through the river surface like the periscopes of a squadron of submarines. They crossed the water single file, soon regained their footing, and one by one emerged to their full height on the opposite shore, their wet bulks gleaming darkly. Across a narrow strip of sand lay the next arm of the river, which they also had to ford to reach the juicy reed fields of the bog beyond, but in the very centre of this stream a tight cluster of thirty or forty hippos formed a living island. One of the hippos, perturbed by the sudden appearance of the elephants, raised his head and blared a sequence of ominous bass tones into the quiet morning. The elephants flapped their ears, raised their trunks, spun around, and ran off in the direction from which they had just come. In their unseemly haste, they resembled agitated fat men whose braces have broken and who are struggling to keep up their speed, their dignity and their trousers. The waters seethed and foamed as they crashed once more into the flood. Back on the far shore, they rested from the excitement and exertion of two crossings. A full half-hour later they made a fresh start, but this time they walked about a hundred yards upstream to avoid the hippos, and only then crossed both channels to the longed-for reed fields.

Toppling Trees

The biggest of the six bulls, standing at least twelve feet high, headed for an acacia tree with a broad umbrella-like canopy. When he reached the tree, he stopped and craned his neck, and his trunk shot up to the tangle of branches like the telescopic ladder of a fire engine. He had to stretch mightily, even standing on tiptoe (so to speak) on his right foot, to bridge the last inches to a branch whose lowest tips he finally managed to grab with his two trunk fingers. He tugged at the branch, screwed the tip of his trunk around the twigs to get a better hold, pulled a little more, wound his trunk a second time around the foliage — much like winding a dog leash around one's wrist — and then, firmly gripping the boughs he had twisted into a rope, pulled with all his strength. The rope resisted only for seconds; then a portion of the treetop came noisily crashing down.

The elephants immediately threw themselves upon the fresh greens. In no time the torn branches were stripped clean and the lead bull reached for the treetop again. His first try fell short, and he lowered his trunk in preparation for a more strenuous tactic. Clutching the fork of a branch with the tip of his raised trunk, he took the tree trunk between his tusks and pressed his forehead against it with such force that the whole tree began to sway. The elephant pushed, stepped back, pushed again, three, four times. With each assault, the bull bent the tree a little farther before allowing it to swing back. After the fifth push, it swung back no more but arched in slow motion to the ground. The crash shattered the afternoon quiet for miles around. Three more elephants left the tree on which they had been feeding a few hundred yards off to share in the new feast.

For the next hour the elephants were busy, tearing the treetop apart with their trunks, tusks and forefeet, and chewing it up. Only rarely was there some minor trouble, when a low-ranking elephant plucked the choicest greens from under the nose of a higher-up, in which case the stronger animal simply shoved the weaker one aside, causing a chain reaction of rearrangements in the feeding order. But once or twice such an altercation led to serious confrontation, and the higher-ranking elephant would deal his rival a blow with his heavy tusks that made their relative ranks and prerogatives unmistakably clear.

During the previous few weeks the area around Lake Ndutu and Lake Masek had experienced an invasion of perhaps fifty bulls. These two small soda lakes in south-western Serengeti form the beginning of the famous Olduvai Gorge, some twenty to twenty-five miles from Laetoli, an excavation site that yielded the fossilised footprints of prehistoric proboscidians. Under normal conditions, elephants seldom stray into this dry area, but there had been two unusually good rainy seasons, and the water of the swollen lakes may well have attracted the animals. In the succeeding dry period, however, little food was available besides the leaves and twigs of the umbrella acacias, and two months after the "invasion" of the elephants, whole stretches of woodland looked as if an armoured brigade had held war-games there. Trees were broken, toppled, strewn pell-mell across the landscape, and the silence was uncanny, almost oppressive.

The fifty bulls were divided into several gangs. As a rule, only males form the advance guard that scouts new territory; the cows and their young follow later. I once observed such a tree-felling squad for several days. On the first day, the bulls toppled five trees, on the second day six, and another six on the third. They didn't even take turns at the job; almost all trees were felled by the same bull. Unfortunately I could not follow them after dark, for I would have got hopelessly stuck in the tangle of fallen trees. And although elephants do sleep for a few hours after midnight, they spend a large part of their nights searching for food — up to eighteen of every twenty-four hours will be spent gathering fresh greens. "My" group must surely have felled some additional trees at night.

Even trees too huge to be uprooted often fall victim to the elephants, hollowed out or girdled by their tusks. In Tarangire National Park, there is hardly a baobab without a broad ring of bark scraped off by elephant tusks. This species of tree has a particularly soft, fibrous wood that the elephants like to dig out, gouging veritable caves in these bizarre plant-mountains, so that the trees eventually collapse under their own weight. In Tarangire a few years ago, in a stroke of grisly irony, an elephant was killed, his spine broken by the weight of a collapsing baobab.

Swimming in Silence

At noontime, my group regularly went down to their watering place at the shore of Lake Masek. After drinking, they waded into deeper water to enjoy a lengthy bath. The weighty creatures slid under the water; bobbed up again; rolled from side to side, raising their trunks like periscopes above the surface to draw in several cubic feet of air; and slowly submerged again. Reappearing, they shoved and jostled in play and friendly combat, mounting each other, ramming one another with their tusks, rolling over to yield to their opponents' thrusts, pushing each other's heads under the water, and re-emerging to snort the air, only to disappear again in the lake. Their trunks writhed like the tentacles of giant octopuses, sometimes getting tangled into knots, and their tusks glistened like walrus fangs among the waves. When they exhaled below the water, little geysers suddenly bubbled on the surface. One bull, his flapping ears whipping up a small storm, trumpeted at a tiny grebe that wanted to fish in the murky flood under the elephant's nose; the agitated waters promised a plentiful catch of fish that day.

From my hiding place in the bushes I had observed the bulls enjoying their bathing for quite a while. As the animals lumbered still farther out into the lake, I was suddenly seized by the spirit of adventure. I yearned to swim with the elephants. Dumping my clothes in the car, I snatched a camera and one of the lighter telephoto lenses and plunged in the water. My lark very quickly turned into strenuous work: I had to keep the camera dry, and that left me with only one arm and two legs for swimming. To get close to the elephants, I had to swim about seventy yards — admittedly a modest stretch, but one that, with the weight of the camera, seemed considerable. The closer I came to the splashing behemoths, the more the camera weighed me down. Only a few more yards. My lungs burned as I tried to catch my breath. I forced myself on — Even if I should drown, I wanted those pictures.

I somehow managed the last few yards that brought the animals within my camera range. But the toughest part was yet to come: I had to tread water with exhausted legs while using both hands to adjust the camera. Finally the water appeared more or less horizontally in the viewfinder. The elephants swam past the focused lens. The picture looked sharp. The animals seemed excitingly near. I pushed the button — two, three times — then I gave up. I could no longer move my legs, my arms felt leaden. I had to lie back to catch my breath. Luckily the elephants, ten or twelve yards off, did not take unfair advantage and try to sink me and my equipment. Though they occasionally glanced at me, they seemed to take me for one of the puffed-up ducks cruising nearby. By good fortune, a dead tree was sticking out of the water a short distance away. I found a fork in it for my camera and, feeling tons lighter, clung to it for a few moments. The elephants continued to romp in the water with noisy delight.

After a brief rest, I felt mysteriously drawn to them and wanted to experience them at closest range. Leaving my camera behind, I was able to use both arms to swim towards them. I felt much stronger. Ten more yards, eight, seven — then, suddenly, the elephants noticed me. Like cobras obeying a snake charmer's tune, their trunks came out of the water. But as I had approached against the wind, they were unable to pick up my scent. I held still until they retracted their probing trunks. Perhaps they took me for another big duck, or even a goose. Slowly, cautiously, I pushed closer. I felt elated. Here I was, swimming with wild elephants, almost close enough to touch them. I lost all fear. I felt free, exhilarated. At the same time I was keenly alert and watched the animals' every move. Without a sound, I slid another yard closer. The bulls rolled phlegmatically along. Suddenly, the elephant next to me raised his head and stared at me. Then he thrust his trunk out of the water to suck in some air. His probing eyes kept searching. He seemed vaguely displeased. The splashing stopped abruptly. The other bulls eyed me mistrustfully. I found myself nearly encircled by the now-silent creatures. The elephant in front of me seemed to ponder whether his trunk would be long enough to grab me and hold me underwater. I didn't wait for his decision. Slowly, and as quietly as possible, I backed away, keeping a careful eye on the bull. Gaining yard by yard, I finally put a safe distance between me and the elephants. Feeling weak at the knees, I swam to the dead tree, picked up my camera and pushed back to the shore. I was glad when I reached firm ground.

Fatal Wounds

Only the biggest and strongest bulls are able to push over trees. Cows, on the other hand, use a totally different method to attack them, but one that in the long run is equally devastating.

A cow and two calves, one four and the other perhaps eight years old, were standing under an acacia tree. Using one tusk as a lever, the mother pried a strip of bark loose until it was long enough for her to grip it firmly with her trunk. Then, pulling steadily, she peeled off a layer about two yards long. The two youngsters worked in similar fashion, trying hard to rip off some of the tough strips. But they lacked strength, and their tusks were too short to inflict more than a few small scratches upon the tree. Still, they were learning to imitate their mother and to appreciate the taste of bark. When the threesome strolled off two hours later, they left behind a fatally wounded tree. Although the rainy season had already begun and vegetation abounded, elephants were attacking increasingly large numbers of trees. At this time of year the fibrous strips of bast seemed to be a juicy addition to the elephants' regular diet, although they contributed less nourishment than the three animals could have gathered within the same two hours had they eaten grass and foliage. The elephants seemed to peel bark mainly during the hot midday hours, when they prefer to remain in the shadow of trees. Perhaps they were bored. Or perhaps they found bark a handy substitute for grass and greenery while the blazing sun kept them from grazing.

Four days after I first saw a cow stripping an acacia, I met another group of cows and calves enjoying their siesta under a large tree. While the others dozed, the lead cow busily peeled off long ribbons of bark. Filaments of bast had been ripped off the wood all the way up to a main fork in the trunk, and two- and three-yard-long strips were dangling above the elephants like ropes from the mast of a ship.

A little while later, the cow lost interest and the animals began to wander off. Only a young bull remained. He fished for the bark, clutched the end of a strip, pulled, lost his grip, reached up again, playfully set the jumble of bast strips swinging all at once like bell-ropes, and then, pulling one strip far enough down to catch it between his teeth, sunk to his knees to tear it off with his weight. The tough fibre resisted. Undaunted, the bull began to pull a second time. Again the strip slipped out of his grip. The ardent tug-of-war went on for ten to fifteen minutes. Despite his clumsy bulk, the young bull in his exuberance reminded me of an oversized cat clawing for threads of yarn.

Elephants are surprisingly versatile and inventive. While they can condemn a tree by attacking the top, or by stripping the bark, or simply by pushing it over, some pachyderms prefer to get at the root of the matter. One noontime, I came across a cow patiently digging out a massive rootstock. Her left tusk was missing (possibly lost in a similar endeavour), but she used her right tusk as a gigantic weapon to ferret out the recalcitrant root – at first without success. She persisted. Having kicked the surrounding earth loose, she seized the stock with her trunk, slipped her tusk underneath it as a lever, and tried as hard as she could to prise it up. The wood groaned, but held firm. The cow repeatedly kicked the root with the front edge of her front foot, then angled and squeezed the foot underneath it and pressed forward. The wood creaked from the strain, but still failed to split. Next she placed the same foot on the other side of the root and drew it towards her. Again, the wood moaned. Again, she attacked with her tusk. A piece of root was laid bare; she kicked the earth loose at both ends of it. After twenty minutes of relentless exertion, she jerked the root from its anchorage. Holding its free end between her teeth, she removed the tough outer skin with her trunk. Having peeled the choicest part like a banana and devoured it, she carelessly discarded the rest.

Liquid Glass

The noon heat weighed on the lake like liquid glass. Soundlessly, the sun hammered its rays into the sand. Five bull elephants, sand crunching under their steps, approached the shore, used their trunks and front feet to dig hollows into the soft ground, and then waited patiently for water to collect in the wells. The leisurely drink took one, perhaps even two hours. Finally, they waded knee-high into the lake, stopped and stood, dozing as the shallow waves lapped around their legs. After a while, the coolness of the water revived their playful spirits. Two bulls suddenly intertwined their trunks, locked tusks, and tried to push each other aside. The water splashed high around them, covering their bodies with a dark, glistening veneer.

This water battle was too good to miss, so I drove as close to it as possible on the sandy shore. One bull resented the disturbance. Without warning, he came rushing at me through the flood, ears spread like the sails of a frigate, pushing a huge bow wave before him. I didn't move. Enveloped in foam, he reached shore barely ten yards from my car — and then skipped around. After pacing nervously back and forth and jerking his erect head angrily at me, he withdrew, his spectacular attack petering out by the water hole he had dug a short time earlier. Unimpressed by their comrade's fierce sally, the other bulls strolled stolidly back to shore. Another stop at their drinking places, and they disappeared into the tall shrubs surrounding the sandy shore.

A few days later, in the same area, I met a lone bull weighed down by an enormous pair of tusks. He was loafing through the afternoon, plucking a tuft of grass here, a few leaves from a shrub there. Then under a tree he found some fruits, obviously to his liking, for he thoroughly scanned the ground under the branches. He found only a few of the olive-green, plum-sized delicacies; others before him had conducted a similar search. But he had a solution: he took the tree trunk between his tusks and shook it. Plums rained down. With great deliberation, he collected his harvest, groping along the ground with his trunk until he found a fruit, taking it between his two trunk fingers, and shoving it into his mouth. The tip of his trunk shuttled steadily between ground and mouth. Often, with a flick of its fingers, he would flip a fruit into his gullet from about ten inches' distance, a time-saving trick he mastered with ease. It took him half an hour to gather the crop. He shook the tree again but this time he merely picked up a dozen or two and lazily went on his way.

33

Monolithic Force

The sun had climbed half way up the eastern sky. It was still early in the day, but a group of elephants had already gathered by the river and were drawing up water with their trunks in long draughts to quench their thirst. Then they ambled one by one over to an enormous tree whose foliage formed so vast a roof that all twenty-eight giants could rest in the shade beneath. A tribe of green monkeys frolicked in the sweeping branches, swinging down by their tails and ranting and raving at the uninvited guests below. They barked and twanged and hollered in every possible pitch, according to their size. Soon, the pachyderms, too, were growling and trumpeting. The squad rose, circled furiously once around the tree, then quietened down again. What had disturbed them was a second group of elephants passing by, a short distance away, on their way to the water. The monkeys kept railing, but without the slightest effect on the elephants.

Some calves were sleeping between the legs of the adults, their breath whipping up the dust at the end of their trunks. One of the cows found a crooked stick, about two yards long, which kept her occupied for quite a while. She placed it across her tusks, raised it over her back, and swung it around with such abandon that she finally knocked a calf over the head with it. The calf grabbed the stick and pulled as hard as he could, but was no match for the cow and quickly lost the tug-of-war. Then the cow dropped her toy, picked it up again, dangled it over her back, threw it aside, and picked it up a second time after a short interval. And so it went on, until she discovered by accident that the crooked stick fitted precisely under her chin. As if resting her head on a pillar, she leaned on the stick, holding this position for two or three minutes before finally dropping the stick and proceeding to massage one of her earlobes with her trunk.

On another occasion an elephant cow was standing next to me, eyes closed, head similarly propped on a forked branch. She remained in this position for a full ten minutes. Young elephants, too, enjoy playing at length with all sorts of sticks, from the flexible twigs of shrubbery to tree branches almost too heavy for them to lift. The elephant's pleasure in manipulating large and heavy bulk material has been put to good use for centuries, particularly in Asia, where elephants used to serve – and in a few places still do – as living cranes in lumberyards.

Soon the herd left their resting place and trotted southwards through luminous woodlands. After a lengthy march, the lead cow guided them to a pool replenished during a thunderstorm three days earlier. Two Nile geese had alighted at the edge of the pool, but quickly retreated with much clucking and wing beating, yielding to the superior force of the grey colossuses. As the elephants had already had their bath for the day, only their young rolled briefly in the wallow; the older animals continued on their way after taking perhaps a shower or two with their trunks. Some stragglers in the herd met the two Nile geese again, who were waddling back to the pool to reclaim their territory after the passage of this mammoth force.

Order and Law

Elephants live in a matriarchal society. A lead cow heads each group, and several such groups form a larger federation in which all members are bonded by varying degrees of blood ties. As females usually spend their lifetime within a family unit, these groups often span three generations.

Because of the elephant's huge demand for food – depending on its size, an adult animal digests two to five hundred pounds of greenery daily – families are constantly roaming the land. In the process, they adapt marvellously to local conditions. With the exception of desert regions, every kind of environment throughout Africa is inhabited by elephants. Despite their bulk, these, the largest land animals, even turn up on the slopes of Mount Kilimanjaro and Mount Kenya, at heights well above 13 000 feet; yet, on rare occasions, they can also be found at sea level, near the Indian Ocean for instance.

Water also determines where the herds wander; the animals need to drink at least once a day, and they consume at least three gallons of water at a time. During the several months of the rainy season, their whole existence revolves around water holes, whence they strike out at any time of day or night on long treks in search of food, only to return within twenty-four hours to their watering place.

Their food consists mainly of every kind of plant foliage, but they are quite capable of living almost exclusively on grass for long periods if little else is available. Their need for food is so great that they can hardly afford to be choosy; they nonetheless show distinct preferences for specific plants or fruit. The intoxicating palm fruit, for example, is a favourite. Bananas are another. It isn't hard to imagine the ravages a herd of elephants can inflict on a banana or corn plantation. Formerly, when the local people saw their fields threatened by elephants, they did what they could to scare them off with noise and tam-tams. Later, farmers tried to spoil the robbers' appetite for the forbidden fruit by peppering their behinds with buckshot.

Several years ago, in Kenya, when a herd of more than one hundred elephants advanced from the dry north-eastern plains towards the farm belt of the adjacent highlands, the defenders of this agricultural Garden of Eden used helicopters to crack down on the pachyderms, driving them off their lucrative high-yield paradise with vicious, low-level attacks. For several decades, elephants have simply been – and still are – gunned down by professional sharpshooters.

When puberty sets in, the twelve- to fifteen-year-old bulls are expelled from the matriarchal groups by the females. For a while they follow at a distance, then they join the other bulls. Only when fully grown will they occasionally visit the matriarchs' herds to mate with the cows. Thereafter, whether or not the mating was successful, the bulls go their own way again.

In times of scarcity or stress, many elephant groups band together to form larger herds; no doubt the animals feel more secure in a big herd when fleeing from hunters or after a lead cow has been gunned down. Defending themselves against humans or other predators, they will often put up a united front. One of nature's rarest and most impressive spectacles is a tightly packed wall of elephants – heads high, tusks shining like rows of spears ready for combat.

Elephants show no territorial instinct. Ranges overlap without causing the least tension between groups. Ranges also vary greatly in size, depending on the availability of food and water. In Manyara National Park, with its rich vegetation and plentiful water supply, the average range of an elephant group encompasses less than twenty square miles, but in the western part of Tsavo National Park, an average range measures more than 140 square miles, and in the dry eastern region of the park a range may cover 640 square miles.

Elephant Wedding

A peacefully grazing elephant herd spread out across the sun-drenched plain. Abruptly, two huge bulls charged each other. An angry trumpet call announced the battle. Tusks clashed, trunks tangled like wrestling pythons as the elephants tried to push each other aside. Twisting their heads, they shoved and pressed, punched each other with their tusks, disentangled themselves, stared at each other for a second, motionless, then charged again with the ferocity of a Cyclops. Each tried to use his trunk to steady his opponent for the next thrust. Though both animals were roughly the same size, the match quickly proved unequal. The weaker rival yielded more and more frequently, gradually losing ground. The intervals between attacks grew longer. After another duel, the weaker of the two heavyweights not only stepped aside, but had to withdraw altogether to catch his breath. Then he again charged his opponent, a gigantic six-tonner, was shoved around, and surrendered by simply turning around and walking off. The victor pursued him for a few paces, but changed his mind and stopped to pluck a bunch of grass instead.

The oft-interrupted fight had lasted barely half an hour. Both animals came away unscratched. Confrontations among bulls — generally a simple matter of rank — usually end without bloodshed. They occur quite frequently among younger males, competing for privileged positions and subsequently defending these. But among mature bulls fights are rare. I therefore suspected that the violence I had witnessed had something to do with the cows, or, more precisely, with their readiness to mate. Cows remain in heat for three weeks, but they can conceive for only three days. While in heat, they mate with a number of bulls. Actual copulation lasts less than a minute.

Two days later, my guess was confirmed. Several elephant families were grazing along the lake shoreline near the acacia forest. The victor of the earlier duel was passing among the cows, testing their willingness to mate by touching their genitals with his trunk. Cows are seldom in a responsive mood; most of the time they simply ignore male advances. But this time, the grey giant detected positive signs in one cow. He was beside himself with excitement, shook his head, trumpeted, and went so impetuously after the cow that she retreated hastily. But not too far. Less than one hundred yards away she allowed the impassioned bull to catch up with her, put his trunk around her and mount her.

The awesome primeval act of procreation triggered a second, equally dramatic spectacle. Excited, the other elephants ran up to the couple, pressed around, and filled the air with a blaring serenade of shrill dissonance, all the while bumping their heads and twisting their trunks into strange configurations. Startled calves ran around amid the confusion, helplessly waiting for the riotous pageant to end. And at the centre of the commotion, almost motionless, stood the bull and the cow.

New to the Bush

I was driving my car slowly, heading for the edge of a pool where I had noticed a tawny eagle and an African fish eagle who seemed to be fighting over some prey. My Land Rover bumped into a hole, shrieked and stopped. The two frightened birds flew off, leaving behind a few large shreds of skin. When I was at last close enough to examine the dark bundle, I realised that I had made an interesting discovery: an elephant cow had dropped her afterbirth here. She must have given birth recently somewhere in the vicinity. As only the two eagles had spotted the embryonic sack, she must have discharged it merely a short time before. The cow and her newborn could not be far. I determined to find them.

Tall grass and thick brush slowed me down. I stopped frequently, climbing on to the roof of my car to survey the surroundings through my binoculars, but I could see only a few impalas and eventually two wart-hogs scurrying through the thicket. I drove a wide half-circle around the area where I thought the herd might be. After a long period of forcing my way through the dense bush, I suddenly caught sight of the grey backs ahead of me. I cautiously crept closer.

About twenty browsing elephants were spread over a considerable stretch of land. The terrain was so difficult to survey that I couldn't make out more than the heads and backs of the adults, even with my field glasses. I had to manoeuvre still closer. One of the bulls drew himself up menacingly, spread his ears and squinted at me, his eyes full of suspicion. With one of his forefeet, he fretfully scraped the ground. Having waited in vain for him to calm down, I finally tried to steal past him, sideways. To no avail. He came at me like a tank. Ten yards away, he veered off. The strong odour of elephant wafted in my direction. This impressive mock attack was intended to scare troublemakers away.

Since I didn't want to alarm the entire herd, I had little choice but to take his forceful hint and retreat. A while later, I tried my luck again and drove around the herd in another large curve. This time I came within fifty yards of the main group, and was immediately struck by the aggressive stance of one cow who stared at me, ready to charge.

Half hidden in the grass between her legs, and dwarfed by her, was a dark figure. As I attempted to get my car into a better position, the excitable mother cow turned tail. The other animals followed. Not wanting to upset the herd further, I had to content myself with watching them through my binoculars. The cows eventually resumed their browsing. Through a few thin spots in the vegetation I succeeded in catching an occasional glimpse of the newborn, who looked minuscule in comparison to his mother. At one point, he tried to suckle, stretching as high as he could to reach the source of milk hovering overhead. He bent his hind legs a little and lifted a front foot for better luck; but his success was short-lived, for the mother cow, still edgy, urged the herd onwards.

The squadron of grey backs drifted slowly away, bobbing among the green waves of the bush. The herd was excited enough by the birth. So, as I didn't want to cause additional trouble, I remained behind. I hoped that during the next few days I would still be able to land a first by photographing the newborn calf. Elephants, after all, don't grow up overnight.

But I was disappointed. Three, four, five days passed. The terrain in the Endabash region is so complex that I was unable to locate the same group again, no matter how hard I tried. Nevertheless, some weeks later, I had a chance to photograph a calf that was barely a few days old, its hide still hanging like an ill-fitting coat about its shoulders, and sprouting long baby hair like a cactus. The calf seemed somewhat dazed and rarely ventured beyond its mother's legs. Standing under her belly when she took her daily shower, it too got soundly drenched. It had an older brother who drank all its milk. For whatever reason – an inflammation, perhaps – the mother cow denied one of her breasts to the two youngsters. This clearly benefited the older calf, the newborn being obliged to wait its turn.

Elephant calves are born relatively large. Both baby males and females weigh about 270 pounds and measure an average of three feet at shoulder height. These giant infants need about two gallons of milk each day. By the time they are one year old, they barely fit under their mother's belly. After losing their baby teeth when they are two or two-and-a-half, they begin to grow tusks.

This is about the right age for weaning, although it can vary greatly, depending on the tolerance of the individual cow. In most cases, complete weaning comes with the birth of the next calf; but certain cows allow their young to suckle even when they are six, seven or eight years old, and they occasionally nurse two calves of disparate sizes simultaneously.

In contrast to most mammals, elephants' mammaries are located between their forelegs. I once observed a big calf, already endowed with sizeable tusks, protesting vehemently when his mother attempted to educate him — his sharp tusks cruelly poked her between the ribs when he wanted to drink. But when she turned away, he made such a fuss, and so stubbornly followed the cow's every movement to get at her breast again, that she finally obliged. However, his growing tusks would soon definitely prevent him from nursing.

Bulls display sexual behaviour from tenderest childhood and mount each other as well as their female siblings with little regard for considerable differences in size. During their early years, calves are given tremendous leeway within their clan for tomfoolery. Adults and adolescents are willing to put up with a lot of nonsense. Towards evening, when the temperature begins to drop, the youngsters perk up. They elude maternal supervision and gather in little sandbox clubs. I once saw a small calf upset an entire herd with its bawling and carrying on as it ran around between the peacefully grazing animals. Alarmed by the possibility of danger, the cows rallied around the presumably threatened youngster, but the enemy was nowhere to be seen. The calf was merely proclaiming its exuberance. When two family units meet, their respective calves grow particularly unruly. They run to meet each other, greet each other with outstretched trunks, sniff each other, skip around each other — and in no time at all, a scrap has begun.

One such afternoon encounter led to a violent fight between two three-year-olds. The pugnacious young bulls wrestled doggedly, twisting their trunks into impossible knots, bumping their heads and trying desperately to push each other around. Both growled and groaned, slammed their foreheads hard into their opponent's belly and behind, and were so absorbed in pulling each other's ears that they forgot the surrounding herds. Stopping to catch their breath, they suddenly found themselves alone.

The two groups had long since parted and were going their opposite ways. The two hagglers saw them grazing at some distance and immediately gave up their belligerence, leaving their account unsettled, and ran with flapping ears and flying tails to catch up with their kin. One of the two heroes happened to come running in my direction. The sight of my Land Rover seemed to increase his panic. He hollered and charged as if determined to trample the car into the ground, but changed his mind and vented his rage and anxiety on a shrub, knocking off some branches with his rear end, and then stormed at me again, screaming. The other elephants, alarmed, raised their heads and glowered at me. Though I knew myself to be perfectly innocent, I was embarrassed by the fuss. I felt as if I were trying to steal a baby's bottle and suddenly was caught by the child's governess. A youthful cow, probably the sister of the youngster who was charging at me, rushed to her little brother's aid, calmed him down and led him safely back to the herd.

A lot of body contact shapes the mother-and-child relationship of elephants. The trunk, of course, is an important tactile instrument. Calves use their trunks to feel their mothers' bodies, to sample the menu by reaching into their mothers' mouths, and to savour their mothers' smell through these long olfactory tubes. Mother elephants, in turn, use theirs to guide their young and to soothe them when they are excited, either by putting their trunks into the youngsters' mouths or by fondling them — reassuring them of their maternal presence and imparting a feeling of security. Despite or perhaps because of their great physical strength, mother elephants are particularly gentle and kind to their calves. But they are by no means completely unselfish. During long periods of drought, when the rivers waste away and the watering places become dust pans, elephants resort to digging ground wells in the sandy riverbeds. Water collects very slowly in these sand holes. The impatient calves often can't wait, and push their trunks down to the bottom of the wells to drink their mothers' water, often causing the holes to collapse. The mother tries to keep her calf at bay until her thirst is quenched, pushing him or her aside with trunk and tusks, even blocking access to the hole with her body. If the thirsty calf is determined to get his way, the competition can go on for a long time. The calf often succeeds briefly, as the mother throws her head back to empty a trunkload of water into her gullet; but then he is instantly foiled again.

On the whole, however, even these tests of patience remain on a friendly footing. Only once did I see a cow shovelling her calf aside with such an angry scoop of tusks that the youngster screamed in pain. Later I saw that he was bleeding from the mouth. Such violent cases are rare. In general, mothers and older sisters look after the small fry with loving care, as the following incident illustrates.

A calf who had been wallowing in a mud hole to his heart's content couldn't scurry to solid ground. He kept floundering on his slippery feet and sliding back. Finally he squeaked for help. Mother and sister hurried to the rescue, hooked their trunks under his bottom, and hoisted him out.

Fury Displaced

Driving along an elephant path isn't easy. The pachyderms meticulously set one foot in front of the other on their treks, leaving a path hardly wider than fifteen or twenty inches. The dense vegetation of the Endabash region makes following the narrow, curving path especially tricky. The best l could do was to plough through the bush.

I was trailing a group that I had discovered that morning around one of the watering holes and that now, in the early afternoon, was returning to the bush. I kept losing sight of them in the tall shrubbery. Time and again, I had to drive around impenetrable islands of thickets in the hope of finding the group on the other side. I had just forded a riverbed and was slowly forcing my way through a jungle of underbrush that girdled a clump of trees when, suddenly, I found an elephant in front of me.

He sounded his trumpet and stormed at my car, stomping down a few bushes in his path. But within six or seven yards, he stopped and turned instead to attack a young sapling that happened to be in his way. On this innocent little tree he vented the rage meant for my four-wheeled jalopy; his courage had failed him. Now, like a wrestler, he wound his trunk around the thin but resilient tree trunk and dragged it to the ground, trampling it. Then he remembered me, released the tree from his stranglehold, and stared at me. The pliable sapling bounced back into its original position. But the bull renewed his attack on the tree, rubbed his tusk against the wood, wheeled around, trampled the branches with his hind legs, trumpeted, scraped the bark with his ivories, and brought his opponent down a second time. He looked at me intensely from time to time, and the sight of me seemed to revive his fury. Again, he vented his awesome strength on the substitute foe, whose foliage was beginning to hang in tatters. Half-crazed, he circled the tree, flinging his head about, his slapping ears sounding like the cracking of whips. He trumpeted, sent splintering wood flying, and trumpeted yet more wildly. A first-class temper tantrum. I was sweating. With a bit more courage, the bull might have demolished my Land Rover. By now, the tree was uprooted. The bull picked up his defeated enemy, shook it, then tossed it aside. He attacked a few more shrubs in passing, crashed through the bushes and disappeared.

Seconds later, I saw his tusks gleaming between the branches to my left. Once more, he gestured threateningly, but avoided the decisive confrontation and was gone. This time, he didn't return. Only his ranting and raving reverberated throughout the landscape. Again and again I heard trumpet blasts from various directions, then silence.

On another occasion, too, I saw an elephant vent her anger on a perfectly innocent surrogate rather than attack a dreaded enemy. This incident took place in the prolific wilderness of the Endabash region. I was cautiously approaching a gathering of cows accompanied by only a few very young calves — part of a larger herd dispersed throughout a vast area. One cow resented my presence. She shook her head, coiled her trunk up against her chest, and charged at me. Fortunately, within a few yards of my car she lost her courage. After a few indignant trumpet blasts, she stepped aside. For a while, I heard her trampling through the nearby thicket. Suddenly she attacked again from another direction and veered off just before hitting me. She repeated the attacks several times. Her last thrust was abruptly diverted by a rootstock. In a violent rage she tore it out, flipped it over her head and disappeared into the bush.

The other elephants had ignored her display of temper and placidly continued to browse. Only an occasional solitary trumpet indicated that the enraged cow was still spoiling for a fight. And then I heard a clashing of tusks from the direction of her last signal. Cautiously I groped towards the noise. Each time I lost the track and stopped to get my bearings, I again heard the clashing of ivory. At the edge of an arid wallow, I found the cow. She was crossing swords with a huge bull and was obviously having fun. This time, she ignored me, no matter how close I ventured. The two behemoths, tusks locked, were pushing each other back and forth. In the end, the bull shoved the cow aside and encircled her shoulders with his trunk in a typical mating gesture. Now absorbed in passionate games, they vanished into the bushes. The unmistakable agitation of the bull indicated that the cow was in heat, which in turn could explain her earlier repeated attacks. A thunderstorm prevented me from further following the two elephants. With sudden vehemence, a curtain of rain descended, making the search impossible.

A Visitor

One afternoon, I was sitting in my car, hidden between some shrubs at the edge of a wallow. The sun beat down mercilessly and the temperature was nearly 35°C. I felt like a steak being grilled. The elephants were enjoying a cool bath, and I begrudged them every drop of water they squirted on their backs. But all I could do was watch the splashing, spraying and snorting of their pleasurable ritual through my camera.

I was deep in contemplation of the idyllic scene when suddenly there was a soft knock on the Land Rover's windshield. I looked up and was face to face with a snake, gracefully swaying its head on the other side of the glass! While I eyed it in surprise, it hissed a couple of times, showing its black, forked tongue. Having recovered from my initial shock — after all, it wasn't every day that I received this type of visitor on the hood of my car — I bent slightly forward to take a closer look at the reptile. It measured perhaps one-and-a-half yards long and the fine-scaled skin on its back was the colour of a light-green reed; its underbelly was white. I had no idea whether it was a poisonous snake, but it only had to wriggle about ten inches to the right in order to glide through the wide-open rectangle where I had removed the window and frame on the driver's side of the car. Naturally, I wasn't exactly delighted by this thought; for although it was no doubt a particularly beautiful specimen, I had no desire to get too intimately acquainted with a snake.

What could I do? Getting out of the car or starting the engine was out of the question; either would drive away the elephants I intended to watch. The snake's searching head was again knocking on the windshield when I had an idea: I knocked back, in the same rhythm and just as softly. The result was baffling. The snake was as shocked as I had been when it first announced itself. It executed a few deft S-curves, slithered down the hood and disappeared via a crack into the engine. Chances were it wouldn't bother me again. I sighed with relief and concentrated once again on my elephants.

That evening, I reported the incident at the camp. Friend Rashid's dark-skinned face lit up. "That's for good luck," he said, beaming. "We have a saying that goes: 'If a snake visits your hut or tent, it's a good omen; but if a lion does, you're in trouble.'" That made sense. I felt blessed that a snake had mounted my hood and not a lion.

Sensitive Giant

In the southern part of Manyara National Park, the Endabash River has gnawed a gorge into the precipitous wall of the East African Rift Valley. But at the height of the dry season, the Endabash was nothing more than a modest brook tumbling down to the valley and looking quite forlorn as it wound its way around the boulders piled up at the bottom of the gorge. After frothing down the final stretch of rapids, the waters quickly lost momentum and seeped into the ground. In the evenings, the elephants often came from the surrounding brush to drink at this spot. Having trouble moving about because of a badly swollen front leg, a sick bull was camping out in the vicinity of the watering place, the only one he could reach because of his infirmity. He spent his days in the shadow of the shrubs that fringed the foot of the rapids.

I wanted to find an observation post among the granite boulders above the water hole. A park ranger toting a rifle accompanied me on my search. We carefully picked our way around the lair of the sick elephant, who was dozing, and breathing as noisily as a diver drawing air through a snorkel. At the foot of the boulders, I took off my sandals to get a better grip on the rocks. We had barely reached the first ledge when the sick bull broke out of the bushes, got on our trail and limped to the boulder where I had left my shoes. From the safety of our rocky perch, we saw him sniff one of my sandals and, with his trunk, abruptly send it sailing through the air, immediately followed by the second sandal. The ranger was grinning. Though briefly vexed by the cavalier fashion with which the elephant had dispensed with my belongings, I couldn't help suspecting that in the course of several years my shoes might well have acquired a smell peculiar enough to provoke even those whose noses are less sensitive than the long olfactory tract of an elephant. A bit embarrassed, I resolved never again to leave my sandals where an elephant might sniff them. Aside from this episode, our expedition was a success. We found an ideal observation post exactly above the watering place. Yet, as luck would have it, the elephants on that day delayed their appearance until it was too dark for me to use my telephoto lens.

While waiting for the animals, I examined the ranger's rifle and was surprised to read, engraved on the lock, that it was an old Mauser, manufactured in 1909. I was being protected by a carbine from the arsenal of the last German Kaiser's former colony in East Africa, and although I would have preferred to have seen it in an antique shop, I hesitantly asked the ranger whether he knew how to make the imperial contraption shoot. "Oh yes," he answered with a radiant smile, "it shoots like a cannon!" He paused to let his revelation sink in, while I cautiously pushed the weapon aside. Then he added: "But you needn't worry; I have no ammunition."

Experience has taught me — often the hard way — that elephants are extremely sensitive to unfamiliar sounds. The point was driven home when I was involved in the following episode in the Selous region. An island rose from the lake like the rounded shell of an outsized tortoise. On it grew one solitary tree and a few green bushes, in the middle of which stood a single bull elephant. As we approached the island, we turned off the motor of our boat. Ndege, our boatman, silently paddled us close to the shore. Sand faintly crunched under the keel as we beached the boat.

The bull elephant didn't seem to notice our arrival; at any rate, he paid no attention to us. Hiding among the few shrubs that fanned out between our landing place and the place where the bull was standing, I carefully sneaked closer, my camera ready, covered by a ranger who crouched behind me, his rifle unlocked. As we were downwind of the grey giant, I could come within ten yards of him without being detected. Slowly I straightened up, appraising the elephant through a gap in the shrubs. The bull, whose gleaming tusks contrasted with his dark hulk, was gathering fallen fruit with slow and deliberate movements. A perfect picture. I pushed the button on my camera — and the faint click was enough to startle him. He turned his head in my direction, raised his sail-like ears in alarm, stuck up his trunk and sampled the air. It was a pose I could not miss. Because some branches were still spoiling the picture, I crept another yard closer.

The bull turned his head from side to side suspiciously and stared straight at my camera. I pushed the button a second time.
The click was feeble, but distinctly different from the sounds of an African morning. This time, the elephant was upset; and this time, he was also able to determine the direction of the disturbance. He immediately took steps to chase us. Fast ones too! He came storming at me like a tank — a terrifyingly beautiful picture, if only I had had the time to capture it. But my legs ran off with me; I bolted like a rabbit. Clearly the stakes were higher than in the famous fable of the contest between the tortoise and the hare.

Ndege was already hastily readying the boat, and the ranger was running behind me. We were lucky. The bull did not insist on kicking us into the lake — camera, rifle and all. It was enough to have taught us some respect. He stopped short, about ten or twelve yards from the boat. Ndege hadn't had the time to start the motor, and we drifted rather helplessly several yards offshore. The elephant could easily have sunk our fragile craft. Instead he stood at the water's edge, in all his splendour, and stared at us. He was once more the undisputed lord of the island.

View from the Banda

I often spent my evenings sitting on the porch of my little *banda* (hut, in Swahili), watching the stars. At times, I also used the roof of the Land Rover as a private observatory. Not that I was making exciting discoveries — other than the occasional shooting stars etching their fiery trails into the dark sky — but it was fun letting my imagination wander aimlessly among the shimmering dots. Some evenings, I was interrupted by the roaring of lions. Once, on a moonlit night, I could even make out the silhouettes of four predatory felines as they were passing by my veranda on their nightly hunt. Now and then, I heard the twanging voices of birds above me or saw a string of flamingos making their rounds.

During my stay in Manyara I occupied two small rooms provided by the park administration. They were located in the right wing of the small group of buildings that constituted the ranger post. My neighbours, three game wardens, patrolled the park on foot all day. The post was built on an elevation that offered a fine view of the parklands and the lake. About two hundred yards to the right, the Musasa River rushed over a few rapids. Between the river and the bandas ran an elephant path leading into the narrow mountain valley that opened up behind the huts, between two hills. Some evenings, on my way home, I had to drive through an elephant herd grazing in front of the ranger station before continuing on its way to the lush vegetation in the valley. Later, sitting on my porch and sipping my first cup of tea, I could enjoy a rare spectacle: less than fifty yards off, a row of twenty or twenty-five elephants, sometimes even more, would stride past almost in silence, seemingly unaware of the human presence nearby.

One night, I was awakened by soft scratching on the wall of my hut. I went outside quietly and in the beam of my flashlight caught a porcupine searching for leftovers. The animal wasn't the least bit bothered by the light, but kept busily rummaging around, at times only a yard from my legs. When I stepped out of its way, accidentally kicking a trash bin, the clang frightened my nocturnal visitor so thoroughly that it ran off in panic. Long after it had disappeared, I could tell where it was running by the rhythmic rattling of its quills. Another time, I awoke at the sound of heavy breathing and of grass being plucked. From my doorway I saw two elephants raiding the front yard in the moonlight.

Lithe Trunks

A phalanx of grey elephants – twelve in all – was standing along the banks of the Musasa River. At irregular intervals the animals lowered their trunks to suck up water, raised their heads, and, putting their trunks in their mouths, let the water run slowly into their gullets.

Each animal was pouring ten or more trunkfuls down its throat to quench its thirst. Between drinks, a few of the behemoths were squirting each other for the fun of it. Some pressed their two opposing trunk fingers together so that jets of water sprang sideways from the now double opening. Others used their trunks to strafe the river's surface and whip up broad fans of water.

Two calves, less than a year old, simply dangled their hoses in the reddish waves. Obviously trying to imitate their elders, but without understanding the complex mechanism of drinking, they were helpless and impatient. One of them finally hit upon the idea of putting his dripping trunk into his mouth and sucking it – a first step in the learning process that, after much practice, would lead to mastery. The other calf, driven by thirst, lowered his head all the way down to the water to drink directly with his mouth, one hind leg sticking up into the air to counterbalance this difficult, top-heavy position.

Baby elephants are not born with the ability to make full use of their versatile trunk. It takes constant training for them to master the countless possibilities of their nose muscles. The trunk acts as arm, hand, water pump, mud-sling, wind gauge, radar, lumber crane and more, much more. It is a supreme masterpiece of evolution, which, by combining nose and upper lip, developed an organ whose agility is only equal to – and sometimes is superior to – that of the human arm. The vast range of its possible uses, from the precise plucking of a single blade of grass to the toppling of a full-grown tree, results from the interplay of several thousand muscles. The co-ordination of these muscles takes diligent training. Very young calves can therefore often be seen helplessly flinging their trunks about, and occasionally trampling on them.

At the watering place I was amazed by one of the bulls, for he had learned an unusual drinking trick. Like all the others, he first filled up his trunk, then squirted the water down his gullet; but unlike the others, he finished it off with a few flips of his looped trunk, as if to shake his nose empty of the last drop. He repeated the distinctive flourishes after every drink.

The group moved slowly away. Only one bull, perhaps twenty to twenty-five years old, lingered. He knelt down in the water, rolled to the side, completely submerged himself, came up again, and, swinging his trunk, got up; then he prised loose a few chunks of earth, threw some of them over his back and swallowed the others. Standing at the very edge of a small flat ledge that projected into the river, he abruptly began to step so forcefully into the waves with his left forefoot that massive sheets of water spattered against his belly. To keep the waves agitated, he repeated the procedure at regular intervals, constantly shifting position to use a different leg each time. With his hind legs, in particular, he sent curtains of water splashing around him. In between, he stirred the mud with wide, circular swings of his trunk. Then he slid into the water again to wallow in another full bath. Back near the shore, he whipped up a fresh little storm around his legs. In all, he enjoyed more than an hour of solitary fun.

The other peacefully browsing elephants had already crossed through the woods that bordered the river and had wandered out on to the beach – a treeless strip of sand – that girdled the lake. Meanwhile, two further groups of elephants were slowly approaching. When the three groups met, there was a welcoming ceremony of sniffing and trunk-touching. Finally the three families mingled into one herd of perhaps forty or fifty animals of various ages.

Nearby, a wallow marked the spot where the Musasa River flowed into the lake. Two adolescent bulls reached this water hole first and promptly began to collect ammunition with their trunks for a mud-slinging contest, soundly peppering each other with the dirt. As if that weren't enough, the smaller of the two suddenly plopped on his knees and, using his feet and tusks, burrowed deeper and deeper into the mire. The other joined in immediately. As if churning in a huge tub of butter, the two bulls, kicking and rolling, made every blubbering, spattering, burping, smacking or squishing noise imaginable. A few cows led their calves to the wallow. The youngsters flung themselves on their bellies and skidded spread-eagled through the slippery mess, rolled over, smeared their heads with the gooey paste, and slithered their trunks like eels through the muck.

More and more elephants were arriving to coat themselves liberally with mud, as if to spruce up their grey old façades with fresh plaster. The wallow was soon overflowing with bodies — ears, trunks, legs and tusks in wild profusion. A large bull came stalking up and elbowed in as if taking his right-of-way for granted, shoving the two adolescents aside and plopping down, the black slime oozing up around his groin. He, too, rolled over and plastered himself so thoroughly with mud that finally only the whites of his eyes were glinting through a mask of clay. After a while, he laboriously propped himself up like a dog on his front legs, paused, drew his hind legs under him, and heaved himself into an upright position. At last he was standing safely on all fours, his legs looking like pillars of concrete arising from the bog.

The place he vacated was at once taken by a cow and her half-grown young, who joined the general press at the wallow. They left ten minutes later, freshly plastered. After a few steps, the cow stumbled across a short, thick stick, picked it up like a brush by its handle with her trunk fingers, and used it to scratch her chest. Then she carelessly dropped it to concentrate on some tufts of grass.

I have often watched elephants use such tools. On one occasion I saw a bull scratching his flanks with a palm frond. On another, a young cow selected a branch to scrape herself. Time and again, an elephant will accidentally discover that a stick can be an extension of his trunk and will remember the lesson when he happens to see a stick that seems to fit the bill. The use of tools in this way, although not widespread among elephants, certainly demonstrates the versatility of an elephant's trunk.

An old bull once showed me a few interesting variations on personal hygiene. Having thoroughly scrubbed every inch of his body against the rough surface of a termite hill, he dozed off for a few minutes, then gave a sudden start, probably inconvenienced by a tickle in his nose. He slipped his left nostril about six or seven inches over one of his tusks, picking his nose by twisting his trunk back and forth. Then he repeated the procedure, screwing his tusk up the right nostril. I was to observe this method of nose-cleaning many more times and concluded that dust, sand and plant particles must frequently get trapped in an elephant's trunk and irritate it.

Elephants are also severely plagued by ticks, especially in the folds around the mouth, under and on the trunk, and behind the ears. The parasites bore their heads into the pachyderms' skin, which, although it has the appearance of wrinkled leather, is by no means as thick as it looks. Having filled themselves with blood, the "ripe" ticks hang from the host animal like yellow-brown berries. Eventually, they drop by themselves or are crushed when the elephants rub themselves against trees or termite hills after their mud baths. I once watched an elephant trying to remove a tick that had drilled itself into his chin. He delicately grasped it with his trunk fingers and pulled it with care; but he failed in his repeated attempts and lost the tug-of-war to the insect. The bite of a horsefly or one of the myriad tsetse flies can anger a young calf, and clearly the daily mud bath serves above all to provide a protective coating against these vermin and their painful attacks.

Having finished their mud baths, the elephants crossed over to a dead tree. I could tell by its smoothly polished trunk that elephants frequently came this way and never missed the occasion to use the tree for a good scrub. One mud-plastered bull, black as night itself in his slippery splendour, first used the scrubbing post behind his ears; after several rubs, he scratched his right shoulder, then his left; finally he concentrated so vigorously on his rear end that the tree began to sway. A few paces away was another tree, toppled. Its main branch was sticking out sideways at about half the height of an elephant, making it an ideal scrubbing stand. The bull strolled over, laid his head on the branch, and scratched himself under the chin. Then he took the wood between his forelegs to sand down his skin above the breastbone. Gradually, all the elephants came by for an equally thorough massage.

The beauty routine ended when the animals powdered their backs, sides and underbellies with dust, applying the finishing touch to the thick mud crust that would protect them from insects and heat. Using their forefeet, they piled up a little heap of dust, ladled it up with their trunks, and fired it like cannonballs, the dust billowing around them. Little by little, the dust drifted away. The elephants resumed their browsing, pulling bunches of grass from the ground and carefully beating them two or three times against their chests to shake off much of the earth before chewing up the grass.

The sun was sinking. A little breeze blew in from the lake; the day began to cool. The young perked up. Like a gang of feisty teenagers, they began cruising around. One little bull broke away from his peers, flapped his ears, spun like a top, and suddenly blew his trumpet so shrilly it seemed as if he meant to rout a pack of lions. But no one paid much attention. So he ran back to his pals, grabbed one of them around the back and tried to wrestle him down. The attacked elephant deftly extricated himself, wheeled around, and slung his trunk around his opponent's, trying with all his might to force him back. Their trunks were pressed upright, the undersides touching. The little fellows were fighting their first duels using exactly the same posture with which adults settle disputes of rank.

Another calf now discovered a handy branch to play with. He wrapped his trunk around the stick, stood it on its end, kicked it, dropped it, and picked it up once more. His quiet play was soon being watched. One of his companions came up, snatched the other end of the stick, and after a brief tug-of-war the toy changed hands. The winner, however, had little use for it, dragged it a few steps, and abandoned it.

Several cattle egrets were walking among the elephants, catching the insects disturbed by the herd's arrival. Suddenly a small bull, his ears spread, charged into the white birds with such determination that he drove them off — only to see them alight again a little further away. Another calf found a vulture's feather. He put the quill into his mouth and flaunted it for a while. Then he took it between his trunk fingers and swung it like a little flag. But as soon as he spotted two young bulls haggling, he negligently dropped his prize and proceeded in all innocence to mount one of the wrestlers. The victim went down on his knees under the surprise assault and rolled over, which caused him to lose the skirmish up front. His playmates immediately stepped on his flanks in the classic pose of the victor. At last, the beleaguered loser was allowed to struggle to his feet.

Birds, Beetles and Behemoths

During countless rainy seasons the river had gnawed deeper and deeper into the earth. Torrents had created cliffs, and kingfishers had carved their nest holes into the bluff. These colourful insect hunters often perched on the stump of a dead tree that arched out over the water. Now and then, one of the birds, looking like an arrowhead with some red feathers glued to it, shot down to the river. It dipped quickly into the waves, bounced up and darted back to its post — usually with an empty beak. But sometimes a small fish, a dragonfly or a grasshopper would be wriggling in its wedge-shaped bill.

I once watched one of these iridescent dive-bombers carve up a grasshopper I had thought far too big for the tiny bird. It kept beating its prey against a branch until all the unwieldy parts such as the legs and the wings had fallen off. Then it let the insect glide into its gullet, head-first. The grasshopper went down slowly. Finally the bird clapped its bill open and shut a few times. Finished. Another time I saw a kingfisher hunt above unusually rich fishing grounds. Within five minutes of repeated diving, it returned three times with a fish in its bill. After gobbling the third fish, it took time off to carefully rearrange its feathers.

One afternoon, a group of elephants descended to the river valley. Placidly browsing, the animals approached the nesting place of the kingfishers. Two adolescent calves suddenly started a fight. They were shoving and pushing each other closer and closer to the nest openings in the bluff. The stronger bull finally pinned his opponent against the wall. The birds, obviously worried for their brood, flitted and twittered excitedly above the two warriors, who paid them absolutely no heed. In gallant defence of its nest hole, one of the kingfishers even alighted on the back of one of the pachyderms, but to no avail. Fortunately, the elephants did little damage other than rub some sand off the wall of the cliff with their coarse skin. As soon as the fight moved into open terrain, the birds darted to their caves and disappeared through the dark openings. A little while later, they reappeared one after the other, chirping and screeching, and flew to their accustomed haunts in the surrounding shrub where they preened their feathers. The hatchery had clearly survived the upheaval.

A few hundred yards downstream I found another family of elephants grazing along the precipitous riverbank. The matriarch spent considerable time trying to uproot a bush that was partially hanging over the embankment. She proceeded to descend the almost vertical embankment wall, which was at least six feet high. She accomplished this unusual mountaineering feat by lying on her belly and, with her forefeet stretched in front of her, sliding down the steep slope till she felt the ground below her and could lower the rest of her body and her hind legs. Two other members of her clan, convinced that there was no better way, also tobogganed down the incline on their bellies. The rest of the group took a short detour.

My Land Rover was settled like a boulder between the bushes. The elephants approached it without fear and stepped nonchalantly around it. Two cows came particularly close, each leading a calf hardly more than a year old. One of them, a young bull, recognised the car as an object foreign to his environment and wanted to satisfy his curiosity. He stopped briefly, within eight yards of the vehicle, raised his trunk, sniffed the air, took a few steps towards me, stopped again, sceptically swayed his head, swung his trunk back and forth hoping to pick up an explanatory scent, and rolled his eyes, drawing still nearer. Then he plucked up his courage and edged close enough to touch the car with his outstretched trunk. He was still puzzled. But the strange object didn't fill him with undue anxiety, for after a few seconds he walked away with the air of an adventurer returning home after a successful expedition, his self-esteem intact.

One of the bulls spread his hind legs, raised his tail and dropped eight soft balls, one after the other, accompanied by a gushing waterfall. Fifteen to twenty pounds of solid body waste and perhaps two gallons of fluid were being dumped. Throughout the afternoon, the elephants deposited various piles of dung that reminded me of those pyramids of ammunition stacked next to medieval cannons.

The elephant manure attracted hordes of scarab beetles, who burrowed into it and kneaded their own little balls from the stuff. In the vicinity of a termite hill, a beetle was struggling to push up a slope one of his creations that was as big as a tennis ball. He was walking in reverse, using his hind legs to coax the ball uphill. But the going was tough; the ball frequently escaped sideways and rolled back down the slope a little. Nonetheless, the beetle seemed to know exactly where he was heading, and the repeated mishaps didn't faze him. Undaunted, he retrieved the ball each time and rolled it uphill again, following exactly the same route. His Sisyphean labour was crowned with success when he and his round freight finally disappeared into a tangle of roots. A few days later, I saw the same procedure in reverse, when two beetles struggled to transport their newly kneaded dung ball downhill. The female clung to the ball in typical female-beetle fashion, while the male did the rolling and steering. But soon the ball started to roll faster than the male beetle was pushing it. Then the male, too, got aboard, and the dung ball, with two stowaways holding on for dear life, rolled faster and faster to the foot of the slope fifteen feet below, where the male resumed pushing it through the grass before burying it at a nearby spot.

An adult elephant drops about two hundred pounds of excrement every twenty-four hours. A group of ten adults therefore distributes more than a ton of first-rate organic fertiliser across the land each day. From the biochemist's point of view, a large elephant herd is like an ambulatory fertiliser factory and plays an essential part in the metabolism/energy budget within an ecological system. Elephants are known to digest their food poorly. Only twenty per cent of what they eat is actually converted into energy; the remaining eighty per cent is valuable organic waste to be recycled.

The recycling of these waste materials is largely done by the scarab beetles, whose whole existence depends on dung balls. There are more than two thousand kinds of such dung beetles in Africa alone, and some of them specialise in elephant dung. The pachyderms' droppings yield food aplenty for countless hordes of scarabs. Some of them flatten the dung into large cakes; others knead it into smaller balls that they bury in the ground within ten to twenty yards of the source. This activity, repeated millions of times each day, processes tons of manure, breaking it up into small doses and distributing it more or less evenly over large areas, efficiently fertilising the soil of an area. The dung provides the scarabs not only with food, but with nurseries as well. The female deposits her eggs into the dung before the male buries it. The young brood must eat their way through a dung patch before they can see the light of day.

The dung beetle, in turn, is of interest to the monitor lizards in this ecological cycle. One afternoon, I observed one of these reptiles creeping out from under some bushes and heading straight for a pile of dung balls. The lizard measured perhaps a yard from his head to the tip of his tail. Upon reaching his goal, he immediately set about tearing the elephants' souvenir apart with his sharp claws. I was baffled at first, until I discovered that the iguana didn't care so much for the dung as for the beetles housed inside it.

Some days later I came across another monitor lizard. He, too, was burrowing in a dung heap and was so intent upon catching beetles that he didn't hear my approach. My car was already within a few yards of him when he quickly bolted, scurried off as fast as a weasel, and flitted past an elephant who in turn got upset and threatened pursuit. The lizard scurried still faster, splashed noisily into a pool, wriggled across to the opposite shore, climbed the embankment, and disappeared into the safety of the dense scrub.

Natural Enemies

Except for people, who have become their most unnatural predators, elephants have no natural enemies. Mature elephants, that is. Young calves can sometimes fall victim to lions or hyenas. Ordinarily, elephant families keep their calves from ending up between the jaws of a lion pack, but any sick or orphaned calf that stays behind will soon attract the rapacious felines' attention. Several reports of lions attacking young elephants are on record. One comes from the Luangwa Valley in Zambia, where a lion pulled a calf to the ground and killed him with one bite to the throat. The victim's tusks were already nearly a foot long. In Uganda, on the other hand, zoologist C. A. Timmer observed a lioness trying to kill an elephant calf. She ended up impaled on a tusk.

The number of elephant deaths due to predators is so negligible that it is not even listed among statistical causes of death — which doesn't mean that elephants never become the sumptuous repast of lions. Far from being only a hunter, the king of beasts is occasionally a shameless looter of corpses. Early one morning, in a little clearing cut into a palm thicket, I found a lioness busy ripping intestines from the corpse of an elephant cow. The feline must have been feeding on the carcass before the crack of dawn, for her belly was already bulging. I had driven past that exact spot the afternoon before and had noticed nothing unusual. The cow must have died during the night, perhaps of a lung disease that at the time had killed several elephants in Manyara National Park.

I discovered the rest of the pack of lions lying among the bushes a few hundred yards from the dead cow, all of them equally satisfied, lolling about in the morning sun without a care in the world. There would be no need to go hunting for several days to come. When the heat intensified, they retreated into the broad branches of an umbrella acacia, where they rested comfortably until evening. At which point they were ready for a second elephant banquet.

The lions of Manyara National Park love climbing trees and whiling away whole afternoons in the branches. But the trees offer more than shelter from heat and mosquitoes. Occasionally, they also offer refuge from the elephants. Elephants don't care for lions and conversely lions prefer to stay clear of elephants. Many a lion cub has saved his life by fleeing up a tree when pursued by enraged pachyderms.

Parched Land

Thunderclouds had been piling up in the evening sky for days. Time and again, sheet lightning flared through the dusk and hot, still air brooded over the savannah. The arid earth had burst in many places, a network of cracks crisscrossing the ground. Dust whirled up at the slightest breath of air. The last water holes had long since dried up; the mud wallows were baked and crusted, forming strange reliefs. The elephants had to dig their holes deeper and deeper into the sand of dried-up riverbeds for a trickle of water. It took a long time before the holes collected enough to fill an elephant's trunk. The sun had singed the grass; half-withered twigs hung from the trees.

One afternoon, a black wall of clouds rolled in from the east. Lightning flashed, and thunder growled across the plain. The first gusts of wind swept the land, driving dust columns and tangled balls of dead shrubbery before them. The wind carried the smell of rain — the earthy, liberating smell that wells up when a first shower drenches the thirsty soil. A few raindrops fell, bursting in the dust like overripe cherries splattering on the ground. Little dust puffs sprang up where the drops hit the dry earth. The rain intensified. Tiny fountains pulsated everywhere from the ground. Soon the thundershower poured down like a waterfall, flooding the parched land.

The elephants, who had roamed far and wide in search of food among the bushes, now stood tightly packed together as the ground was quickly covered by several inches of water. The animals patiently weathered the cloudburst that came rattling down on them; meanwhile, they filled their trunks with fresh rainwater. Some small calves ran excitedly about. They fanned the air with their ears, swung their trunks, spun around in circles, splashed through puddles, dipped their trunks into the flood, and puffed and snorted exuberantly.

One pit of the wallow had already become a pool. Four calves, one by one, slipped over its frothy edge and down into the fresh bath. They rolled, tussled and wriggled in the mud, stuck their legs into the air, squeaked and trumpeted into the rain, attempted to climb out, skidded, and slid back into the pit. A few adult animals joined in the fun and plunged into the warm rainwater. Two adolescent bulls were wrestling playfully at the edge of the wallow. One of them stepped back, slipped and landed on his backside, paddled helplessly around in the slime, and at last regained his footing. The tremendous excitement that had seized the herd when the storm began gradually subsided. The elephants had quenched their thirst and had enjoyed a heavenly shower. Now they dispersed again to continue browsing in the brush.

I did what I could to dry the several cameras I had used to record these jolly rites of spring. Unfortunately I hadn't expected it to rain on that day and had, as usual, set out without taking along the two side windows that I had removed from the Land Rover to make picture-taking easier. Of course I had been unable to resist photographing the pachyderms during the downpour instead of taking shelter in the rear of the car and waiting for the storm to blow over. As a result, I was soaked to the bone, shivering like a wet cat, and feeling punished for my negligence. But I figured it was a small price to pay for participating in the elephants' rain festival.

The Magic Elephant

The bull was coming at me, ears spread menacingly. Abruptly, within yards of my Land Rover, he stopped and headed for the bushes, head high. The sight of an elephant attacking full sail is so terrifying that most of his enemies will take to their heels at the giant's first steps.

Evolution has endowed the elephant with huge ears not so much to help him intimidate his adversaries, or to equip him with an instrument so sensitive he could almost hear grass grow, but to protect him from heat stroke under the hot African sun. For an elephant's ears represent a highly efficient cooling system. They are shot through with a bundle of large arteries branching off into increasingly smaller blood vessels. When the elephant moves his ears, the fanning motion generates an air current, cooling his blood, which is circulating close to the skin surface. With the help of a transmitter tied around the neck of an elephant that had been tranquillised, Iain Douglas-Hamilton established that the blood pumped into this cooling network through the large artery and the blood leaving the ear through the veins can differ by several degrees in temperature, depending on the elephant's activity. An elephant easily adjusts his cooling system to the changes in his environment throughout the day. He simply has to fan quickly or slowly with his ears. At night, or during the cool morning and evening hours, he doesn't have to fan as much as during the hot hours of the day, which he spends mostly in the shade of trees. In cases of extreme exertion, for instance in flight, he can cool himself further by burping up water from his stomach and using his trunk to hose it over his shoulders and ears.

An elephant's tusks, as well as his ears, possess remarkable features. Constantly worn down by daily use, they grow throughout his entire life. In adult cows, each tusk may weigh 45 pounds on average. In bulls, they can easily weigh two or three times as much, sometimes more. The heaviest pair of elephant tusks on record weighed 225 pounds and measured 10 feet 5 inches and 10 feet 2 inches respectively. They came from a bull shot in 1898 in the Kilimanjaro region. The tusks of Ahmed, a legendary bull who lived in the Marsabit area of Kenya until his death in 1974, and whose life-sized memorial stands guard in front of Nairobi's National Museum, also weighed in at almost 220 pounds each. Unfortunately, this kind of "big tusker" — as it is called in the hunting jargon of East Africa — has become exceedingly rare as a result of the boom in the ivory trade.

Just as there are right- and left-handed humans, elephants prefer to use either their right or left tusk for their daily chores – and their tusks wear down accordingly. In many cases it is possible to tell right-tuskers from left-tuskers by a notch mark immediately above the tip of the more frequently used tusk. These notches, which can be distinctive, result from the elephant's using his tusk as a lever when pulling bundles of grass from the earth. Day after day, grass is loosened with the same well-practised prising motion and pulled across the same spot on the tusk, creating a groove in it that becomes quite deep over the years. Only two-thirds of the tusk, from the tip up, is solid ivory; the hollow third near the root houses the nerve.

Next to an elephant's trunk and the size of his body, his tusks are doubtless his most striking feature. But the teeth inside his mouth are just as interesting and important. In the final analysis, the teeth determine how long an elephant will live. Only one molar at a time can grow in each of the two upper and two lower sides of an elephant's jaws. Constant chewing of food not only wears the molar down, but gradually causes it to lean forward along the ridge of the jawbone while a new molar is growing in eventually to replace it altogether. Only six such sets of molars can grow in during the span of an elephant's life. Once the last set of four molars is worn down, the elephant can no longer chew properly. Even surrounded by the lushest vegetation, he slowly and surely starves to death, an event that normally takes place at the time when he has reached an age of fifty-five or sixty.

An elephant herd constantly emits all sorts of sounds. In addition to the frequent, unmistakable noises of their digestive systems, the animals command a broad and diverse range of grumbles, growls and grunts by which they communicate with one another, individually and from group to group. Searching for food, the pachyderms must disperse over large areas, and in the dense bush they often lose sight of one another; but their low-frequency grumbling and growling enables them to keep in touch acoustically even when they are more than a mile apart. These sounds, or their absence, provide the basis for an efficient warning system: as soon as the animals sense any kind of danger, their growling abruptly stops. An eerie silence ensues. Suddenly, soundlessly, their trunks writhe skyward like S-shaped radars to read the air, and the animals stare mistrustfully in the direction of the suspect disturbance.

Whether the cows will gradually resume their browsing and renew their "conversation" of grumbles, or whether — in the case of serious threat — the herd will flee quietly on the soft soles of their feet, depends on the situation. Unless pandemonium breaks out and they crash through the brush in panic, elephants can leave an area almost inaudibly.

And they can *approach* just as inaudibly, as I discovered by accident. Hidden in the shrubbery of an embankment, I was watching a number of elephants squirting water at one another in a pit about two yards below me. I knew the spot well; it was the elephants' favourite water hole. I had taken up my hidden post before they appeared and had been waiting for them for about an hour. As they approached from the opposite direction, I felt sure that they hadn't noticed me. But the bush was so dense that only a part of the herd appeared in my viewfinder. While changing to a bigger lens, I obeyed a hunch and looked behind me. An elephant cow towered above the shrubs, head held high, staring down at me. She was only about three yards away. Not a sound had betrayed her arrival. The thrilling activities by the water forced me to disregard the cow; I shot many pictures before turning around once more, some twenty or thirty seconds later. The cow had disappeared as quietly as she had come. Curiosity must have driven her to inspect my hiding place at close range.

At the edge of a small pool, the hollow pelvic bones of a dead elephant were bleaching in the sun. Other parts of the skeleton were scattered about. A family group with several young calves came strolling by. The mature animals trotted apathetically past the bones, but the smaller elephants were taken aback, warily sniffed the white hulk, and sidled uncomfortably past the remains. In general, the carcasses of dead elephants seem to attract the living quite strongly. They examine the various pieces closely, seize some of the bones in their trunks, and carry them for hundreds of yards before dropping them again. Tusks seem to fascinate them in particular. Iain Douglas-Hamilton and Simon Trevor have taken films in which elephants extract the tusks of corpses, take them into their own mouths and drag them over long distances.

Studies conducted in the Tsavo area for eight years show that a large number of tusks were found up to half a mile away from the corpses to which they belonged. Too heavy for hyenas, they could have been carried that far only by elephants. This behaviour may well have contributed to the legend of elephant cemeteries.

Since old elephants are old mainly because their last set of molars is too worn for them properly to chew their food, they prefer to stay in swampy areas where grass and plants are juicy and soft enough for chewing even with failing teeth. In the end, of course, they die there and their bones subsequently get spread around by other elephants. Wherever an especially large number of bones happens to be strewn across a swampy meadow, it is easy to imagine a "cemetery". However, it is also possible that the accounts of elephant cemeteries passed on to us by the hunters and adventurers of the last century are based on the remains of herds that perished together in some sort of catastrophe – perhaps a brush fire or a sudden eruption of gases – perhaps as a result of drinking poisoned water or of being killed in a large-scale *battue* hunt. Fantastic legends of elephant cemeteries have often captured our imagination, but such treasure troves of white gold exist only in adventure stories.

Footprints of Time

Any of the observations I have made of elephants could just as well have been made a hundred, a thousand or even a hundred thousand years ago. It was during the Eocene epoch that a creature began to proliferate throughout Africa whose nose gradually grew into a trunk. During the late Miocene epoch, some 5 to 15 million years ago, this "prototype" had already developed into the *Elephas primus*, ancestor of today's only two surviving elephant species – the *Loxodonta africana* (African elephant) and the *Elephas maximus* (Indian elephant). Eventually, more than three hundred kinds of proboscidians – the zoological term for all animals equipped with a trunk – were to develop during the 55 million years since the pig-like *Moeritherium* made its first appearance. Most of them evolved over several million years only to die out because they could not adapt fast enough to ecological changes in climate and vegetation, or because faster-adapting species caused a food scarcity, dooming them to a process of starvation that lasted for hundreds of thousands of years. Only two species of the huge family of proboscidians, which once inhabited most regions of the earth, have survived into the present.

Among the fossilised hominid footprints excavated in 1975 near Laetoli in Tanzania by the late anthropologist Dr Mary Leakey are a few imprints of proboscidian giants. They were made by elephants of the species *Loxodonta exoptata*, and by a *Dinotherium* – a proboscidian whose tusks, contrary to those of present-day elephants, grew from the lower jaw and curved downward. The imprints contribute important circumstantial evidence of these creatures' existence and were left in a layer of volcanic flue ash which, under the influence of rain, solidified into tuff, thus preserving over the millennia a "foot-written" testimony of prehistoric life.

One fine prehistoric day, the plains must have been abuzz with pedestrian traffic, for Mary Leakey's excavations have brought to light a number of traces left by an interesting variety of animals, including those of two beings who walked erect. The parallel footprints of the two bipeds constitute a highlight amongst Mary Leakey's finds. With the help of modern dating methods, it has been established that they are 3.6 to 3.8 million years old. On that particular afternoon, proto-humans walked across the plains free to use their hands: some elephants and another proboscidian were nearby.

A few million years later, I found myself in the same landscape, contemplating their recently uncovered footprints. Despite the African heat, a chill ran down my spine: 3.6 million years seemed a hellishly long time, its depth unfathomable. The prints of the hominids looked for all the world like those of modern-day people that can be found on any sunny beach.

The path from the scientists' camp to the excavation site led past a wallow. A recent thunderstorm had soaked the earth and I noticed that the black mud clearly revealed the huge tracks of a present-day elephant. The ancient and fresh imprints were barely a few hundred yards apart! Yet an infinity separated them. Much has happened during the intervening millennia. From the elephants' point of view the long story of what the hominids eventually did with their freed hands is not a happy one. And the pachyderms were pushed with ever-increasing speed towards extinction.

I recall Hannibal, who mobilised elephants to serve as his army's armoured corps and led them across the Alps. This, and other campaigns they were conscripted to, did the elephants little good. As a military tool elephants fast became obsolete, mainly because in the heat of battle they did not always make a clear distinction between friend and foe. As ivory producers, however, their popularity increased steadily. Unlike the Indian *Elephas maximus*, where only bulls grow tusks, both sexes of the African species are armed with these huge teeth, which have evolved from the upper incisors, as everyday tools or as weapons. When bulls clash over the right to mate with a female in œstrus, they fight with ivory sabres.

Humans have a very different use for the tusks. For centuries the best carvers have sculpted fine works of art out of these smooth cream-coloured teeth. But in the past they were also used for more profane purposes such as making a range of luxury items, billiard balls, piano keys or even buttons. Small signature seals made of ivory, called *hanko*, contributed largely to the sharp decline of elephant numbers during the last few decades. These prestigious emblems of personal identity are widely used in Japan to authorise cheques and official documents. The demand for this early item of international trade proved disastrous. It began by killing off the elephants in North Africa; then, as supplies of "white gold" petered out, the slaughter of elephants spread south of the Sahara. For centuries, ivory was Africa's premier article of export, one that tribes of the interior could exchange for goods from the Orient. Long before the Portuguese, English and other Christian seafarers discovered Africa on their expeditions in search of fame and riches, a lively white gold trade crossed the Indian Ocean from Africa to Arabia and Asia.

But it took the advent of firearms to turn the ivory business into big business. The Arabian merchants who had settled in Zanzibar and along the east coast of Africa begAn to supply their native "collaborators" with modern weapons. Now that it was easier to kill elephants, the booming ivory trade went hand in hand with a booming slave trade. Prisoners taken in brutal attacks on native villages were used to transport ivory reaped in equally brutal attacks on elephant herds. In long caravans, the victims of a greedy trade were driven from the centre of Africa to coastal ports, burdened with a double load – personal misfortune and heavy tusks. It was a lucrative business.

Tippu Tib, a legendary slave trader of his time, once returned with twenty-seven tons of ivory from one of his safaris – safaris that averaged about ninety days of enforced marching from the interior to the Indian Ocean. To judge by the weight of the booty, he required more than a thousand slaves as carriers. With the colonisation of Africa, white elephant hunters helped swell the ranks of the ivory suppliers. Statistics reveal the extent of the devastation: towards the close of the nineteenth century, roughly 850 tons of ivory were shipped to Europe each year. The most conservative estimates suggest that more than one million elephants were killed between 1830 and 1930.

For several hundred thousand years, the elephants had lived peacefully, undisturbed from generation to generation. But once caught in human history, their fortunes declined dramatically. South Africa, for instance, bragged a century ago of having "rid itself" of elephants. In the rest of Africa, the elephants' time has run out more slowly; but nonetheless their end is approaching with accelerating speed. Since the turn of the twentieth century, Western civilisation and technology have been encroaching on all available space even in the remotest areas of the African bush. Elephants are already crowded out of vast areas of their original territory, and their remaining habitat is severely threatened by the advance of land- and profit-hungry people.

A night as soft as velvet covered the vast African bush. Mysterious bird calls pierced the silence from time to time. A hyena howled in the distance. Somewhere, a few jackals barked shrilly at the moon, whose yellow light cast ghostly shadows across the landscape. Some giant figures emerged from the dark and slowly stepped into a clearing. Others followed, several smaller shapes and then larger ones again. White sabres shone in the moonlight, gleaming against the dark silhouettes – ivory! Under cover of night, a herd of elephants had come out of the bush and was heading for the river to drink. Unhurried despite their thirst, the animals walked at a calm, measured pace along a well-worn elephant path that wound its way like a narrow road through the brambles.

The watering place was a broad, desolate strip of sand at the edge of a lazily rolling river. The animals came pushing through a sunken pass to the embankment. Suddenly shots rang through the night. Four massive figures collapsed. The dry cracking of a new round of shots mingled with the trumpet calls of the terrified behemoths. Panic seized the herd. But flight was difficult in the narrow hollow.

The animals butted into one another, falling over and trampling their dying comrades, to be felled by bullets in their turn. Only a few escaped, crashing madly through the undergrowth. As soon as the noise died down, the poachers crept out of hiding. With axes and machetes, they cut the tusks from the dead elephants' jaws, taking only the ivory. Their filthy butchery kept them busy for the better part of the night. Then the leader gave a signal. A truck that had been waiting at a distance rolled up and the bloody tusks were loaded. A short while later, the engine started humming and the truck began to move; the poachers disappeared with their booty into the night. At last, the droning of the engine faded away. The silence hung like a shroud for the dead.

In the morning vultures would be circling above the massacre, for some thirty elephants lay on the ground, including calves too young to bear tusks. Dead. Finished. Flies would soon swarm on the corpses. Africa's friendly giants are defenceless against modern weapons, and in many of the continent's remaining elephant areas, they have been decimated by organised poachers during the seventies and eighties. In the past, the poachers were interested in the elephants' meat as well as their tusks, but ivory has become so valuable that they are now exclusively after the tusks. Mountains of elephant flesh are left to rot. Some gangs of poachers are equipped with semi-automatic weapons, usually taken from some military arsenal and readily available on the flourishing black markets. Other gangs go hunting with more traditional gear, such as poisoned arrows and snares. I once found a steel snare in the middle of a national park. A few weeks later I saw a bull with only half a trunk. He had lost the other half in a snare. In some regions, the killers poison fruit or water holes to kill elephants; they also trap smaller herds in carefully controlled bush fires.

Some governments protect their country's wildlife – and this of course includes their elephants – with great determination. Speaking for many African nations, Julius Nyerere, the first President of Tanzania after independence, expressed his government's commitment to the protection and preservation of African wildlife in his famous Arusha Manifesto:

The survival of Africa's animal world is for all of us a matter of great significance. These creatures and the wilderness they inhabit are not only an important source of wonder and inspiration, but are also an integral part of our natural resources, of our future livelihood, and of our well-being. By holding our animal world in trust, we solemnly declare that we shall do everything within our power to ensure that our children and grandchildren too, will be able to enjoy this rich and precious heritage. The preservation of wild animals and their environment calls for specialised knowledge, skilled workers and financial support, and we urge other nations to share with us in this important task whose success or failure will affect not only the African continent but the entire world.

Unfortunately, the years since then have shown all too often that good intentions are rarely followed by good deeds. Idi Amin allowed soldiers of his army to go elephant hunting with machine guns, whilst in the Central African Republic, "Emperor" Bokassa – before his fall – was a partner in a company whose enormous profits were made by selling his country's ivory harvest abroad. Guerrillas in Angola, Mozambique and Ethiopia have decimated their elephant populations and traded the ivory for weapons. Some governments and park adminstrations have done what they could to stop this illegal sell-out of elephants. Wildlife patrols and gangs of poachers often fight pitched battles, and many a ranger has paid with his life for his courageous stand against the gangsters, who are usually better armed. Lack of funds means the patrols are often ill-equipped, but even with the best weapons and equipment, it would be hard to win the guerrilla war for ivory. The lure of high profits remains irresistible. Both the business interests that back them and the areas where the gangs operate are too vast and difficult to survey.

Footprints into the Future

The fate of the elephants, past and future, is largely the result of two factors. The first is ivory — better known as "white gold" — and its market value. The second factor has to do with an alarming set of numbers which reflect a deadly threat not only to the elephants but to wildlife as a whole. It took man more than a million years for his numbers to reach one billion, a monumental event which slipped by completely unnoticed about two hundred years ago. Doubling to two billion inhabitants was achieved within a tiny fraction of that time, by about 1930. A few decades later the global economy faced the enormous task of feeding four billion people. Today we are close to six billion earthlings, with more than ten million new citizens arriving on the planet every month. Optimists hope that the growth of the human population might level off near the ten billion mark, which is likely to be reached before the middle of the next century.

Scientists in turn have estimated that at the time when Columbus discovered America around ten million elephants roamed Africa. By the end of the last century their numbers had been more than halved, but there were still several million pachyderms crisscrossing the continent. When, in the later decades of this century, prices for raw materials soared in the wake of the oil crises, those for ivory also took off. Excited by the dollar signs flashing on the world market, gangs of poachers swarmed into the bush. As a result, the elephant population crashed below the one-million mark during the mid-eighties. The CITES ivory ban temporarily stopped the slaughter, but under pressure from southern African countries, the ban was recently lifted. Despite a handful of new regulations, ivory can now be legally traded once again. Still one can hope that about half a million elephants will be around to greet the new millennium.

Of course, the two sets of population figures are related. The crash of the one has been caused by the exponential growth of the other. The human population explosion has not only helped to create mega-cities like Shanghai, Mexico City and New York, it has also scattered people all over the globe and forced them to colonise even the most marginal stretches of arable land. With the growing number of people living in Africa, the number of elephants has shrunk dramatically and so has the size of the elephants' land. Modern states have sprung up in areas where, millennia ago, elephants laid the first network of footpaths, travelled upon not only by many other animal species, but also by early man on his way to conquer the world. Luckily, here and there, governments have reserved parts of that land for the original inhabitants. Today only a small proportion of the total population of African elephants survive outside national parks, game reserves and other protected areas.

Yet elephants need vast stretches of land to thrive. The biggest land mammals in the world also have the largest appetites. An adult elephant is capable of processing up to a quarter of a ton of greenery every day. Add 20 gallons of water or more, multiply these quantities by the individuals in a population and, given time, you end up with a major impact on the environment. This explains why a herd of these giant plant-eaters must continually be on the move. If they stayed for too long in a particular valley or forest range the supply of fresh shoots and green leaves would dwindle rapidly. Ideally, the feeding grounds of a population are so extensive that the elephants crop only that part of the fresh growth which is left over after accommodating the food requirements of the other herbivores. Otherwise the plant stock will be reduced and the growth rate of green matter will decline. Elephants roam over huge areas, knocking down trees here, ripping off branches there and plucking out trunkfuls of grass along the way. A healthy elephant population indicates a big, healthy eco-system that can sustain the hunger and thirst of these giant eaters over a long period of time. Protecting elephants means protecting an eco-system and a huge chunk of wilderness. It means protecting the whole pyramid of wildlife.

There is also an economic side to the issue. African wildlife —
especially the elephant — is now more and more concentrated in
national parks and game reserves. Thousands of visitors from all over
the world make the pilgrimage to these wilderness areas each year.
For the tourist industry this stream of people turns the white gold
into the dollar equivalent of real gold. There is no need for alchemy.
Season after season, elephants and their majestic tusks attract
hundreds of thousands of visitors to Africa, injecting millions of
dollars and other much needed foreign exchange into the national
economies.

It is to be hoped that more of the revenue raised by tourism will
find its way down to the villages surrounding the remaining wildlife
areas and help improve their schools, medical facilities, transport
and other much needed infrastructure. Adequate financial input at
a local level would help convince villagers that wild animals, even
elephants, are not so much rogue agents of crop destruction as
valuable natural resources which need to be protected — if not out
of respect for their creator then purely in consideration of their
economic value. It must also be hoped that local politicians, armed
with the arguments of their national leaders, so persuasively
articulated by Julius Nyerere in his Arusha Manifesto — and backed
by the strong economic arguments of the tourist industry — will
be able to achieve consensus amongst their peoples in support of
the long-term protection of wildlife in general, and elephants in
particular. In the constant struggle to balance conflicting interests,
the bundles of tourist dollars coming in each season might tip the
scale in favour of elephants.

The half a million elephants living in Africa today could carry about
10 million pounds of ivory into the next century. At the generous
price of $50 (US) per pound (a figure close to the peak rates before
the last ivory ban came into effect), this would set the potential
market value for a one-time sell-out of all African ivory at $500
million. The amount may seem huge in a continent where many

people struggle to earn one dollar a day, but compared to the money accrued by the tourist industry, half a billion dollars is not excessive. We can look at just one country, Tanzania. There are other countries with much bigger tourist industries, but in this East African state, the government plans to double the number of overseas visitors within the next few years to about half a million. If this target is achieved, up to $500 million would be injected into the economy each year.

Elephants could not take all the credit for this substantial income but they certainly provide a heavyweight factor in the bundle of tourist attractions that drive the safari business. Tourism is the fastest-growing section of the global economy and Africa can expect to continue receiving a fair share of this growth. Seen from this perspective, protecting elephants could become one of the best investments a country could make. In the coming decades, living elephants will earn a nation such as Tanzania more foreign exchange than all the ivory extracted from dead elephants over the last few centuries put together. "Save the elephant" could become an investment slogan, as well as an appeal to the consumers of the world not to buy ivory.

Whether or not to ban the sale of ivory has been the subject of many heated debates. The different sides have very different long-term interests. But there is a more immediate problem, for which solutions can be found by looking at the closely monitored status of the elephant populations. Large herds living in the wild can survive into the twenty-first century only if the governments of the countries in which they live come up with drastic measures for their protection and can muster enough popular support to enforce these measures. In most cases, however, the cost involved will prove prohibitive for the strained budgets of developing nations.

Elephants, with the rest of Africa's wildlife, constitute a unique world heritage. Even the people of rich industrial nations have a moral claim to it. But anyone who lays a moral claim to such a heritage should be willing to help pay to preserve it. The developing countries can hardly be expected to defray the cost of a worldwide heritage for the chief benefit of tourists from affluent societies. Most people in Africa cannot afford a single visit to one of their parks. These "national" parks should become "international" parks, certainly in terms of their financial support. They have long been international in their attendance. Many environmentally orientated organisations – World Wide Fund For Nature, or the Frankfurt Zoological Society to name a few – have for years made great efforts to support national parks and to make many of their programmes possible. If some public funds from the ecology budgets of technologically advanced countries were made available, the various aid efforts could perhaps be consolidated to form a network of sponsorship for Africa's national parks.

Along some of the boundaries between the pitifully small islands of elephant land and the modern world, fierce battles are fought night after night. Farmers protect their crops against marauding elephants with a variety of devices including drums, fires and booming symphonies of clattering tin pots and human voices. But if a five-ton bull, alarmed by all the strange noises and movements gets panicked into attack, there is little that can stop him. Fires won't, noise won't, stones and arrows won't, and the muzzle-loaders or World War I carbines which some of the villagers are armed with will not do much stopping either. There are casualties on both sides. Whole crops are steamrollered in one night; the lives of farmers, their families and friends are lost. Elephants get killed as well. The farmers need to be compensated for the crop damage inflicted upon them and even more so if the conflict betweeen humans and elephants brings tragedy to a village or family. Any conservation strategy agreed by governments and international bodies has to accommodate these needs in the fairest way possible.

Meanwhile, the intractable problem of the human population explosion looms large in the background. The last decade of the outgoing century saw, amongst others, an oil war. In the next century, which will see yet another doubling of the world population, wars are likely to be fought for an even more basic resource: water. The animals – especially the bigger ones and foremost the elephants – now protected in national parks, game reserves and other remaining wilderness areas, might easily fall victim to those wars and civil unrest, or simply to the desperate need for land of hungry people.

If humankind cannot get this explosion under control, by means of its own intelligence and ingenuity, life on earth will become precarious. Needless to say, under those circumstances today's elephants will soon become tomorrow's legend. These peaceful, wonderfully bizarre giants, created over fifty million years of evolution, so hopelessly outdated and outpaced by modern times, will become an excellent and not easily overlooked indicator of our ability to solve this ultimate problem.

African Elephants

African elephants can easily dominate the landscape, especially when they pull together for a threat display. Big bulls have no natural enemies to fear and a mock charge is generally sufficient to scatter any animal daring enough to irritate these giants. Nevertheless herds gather together when alarmed and can show signs of insecurity and fear. Cows become very distressed when they sense any danger to their calves, and are always alert and ready to defend them.

It took evolution thousands of generations to forge nose and upper lip into a most versatile body-part: the trunk. Free of bones and joints, it can reach most areas of the body. While its strong muscles allow it to handle the heaviest of objects, it can be controlled with enough precision to pick up a mere olive-sized fruit. To probe for smells it extends into an S-shaped tube testing the air, to scratch the jaw it curls around the tusks. This long water-hose, pump, crane or trumpet can pluck leaves or pull out bundles of grass, making it a multi-task organ, comparable to the human arm.

The eyes of elephants are rather small in comparison to their body size, and adorned with long eyelashes to protect them from flies and other intruders. Their vision is strongly aided by the sensitivity of their hearing and touch. Their large ears are perfect sound traps able to catch long-distance calls emitted at low frequencies by other elephants several miles away. For animals living in herds, communication is crucial. In a group there is always some rumbling and grumbling going on, particularly when the animals are feeding or taking their daily bath at a water hole. One can "hear" when the matriarchs have sensed danger by the sudden silence that mutes the group.

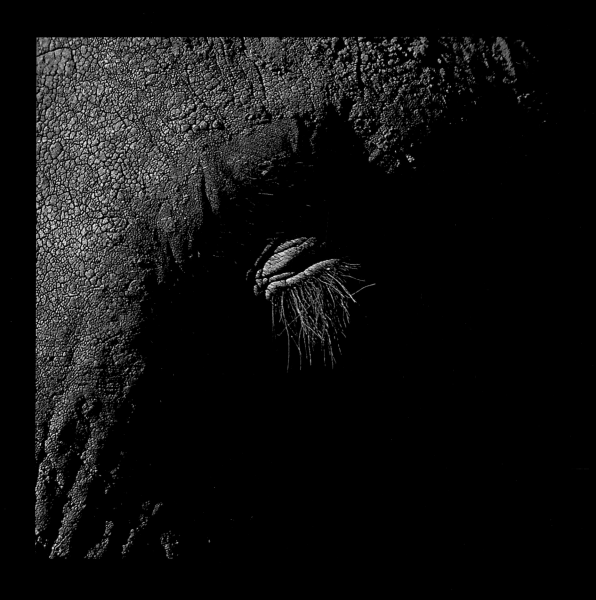

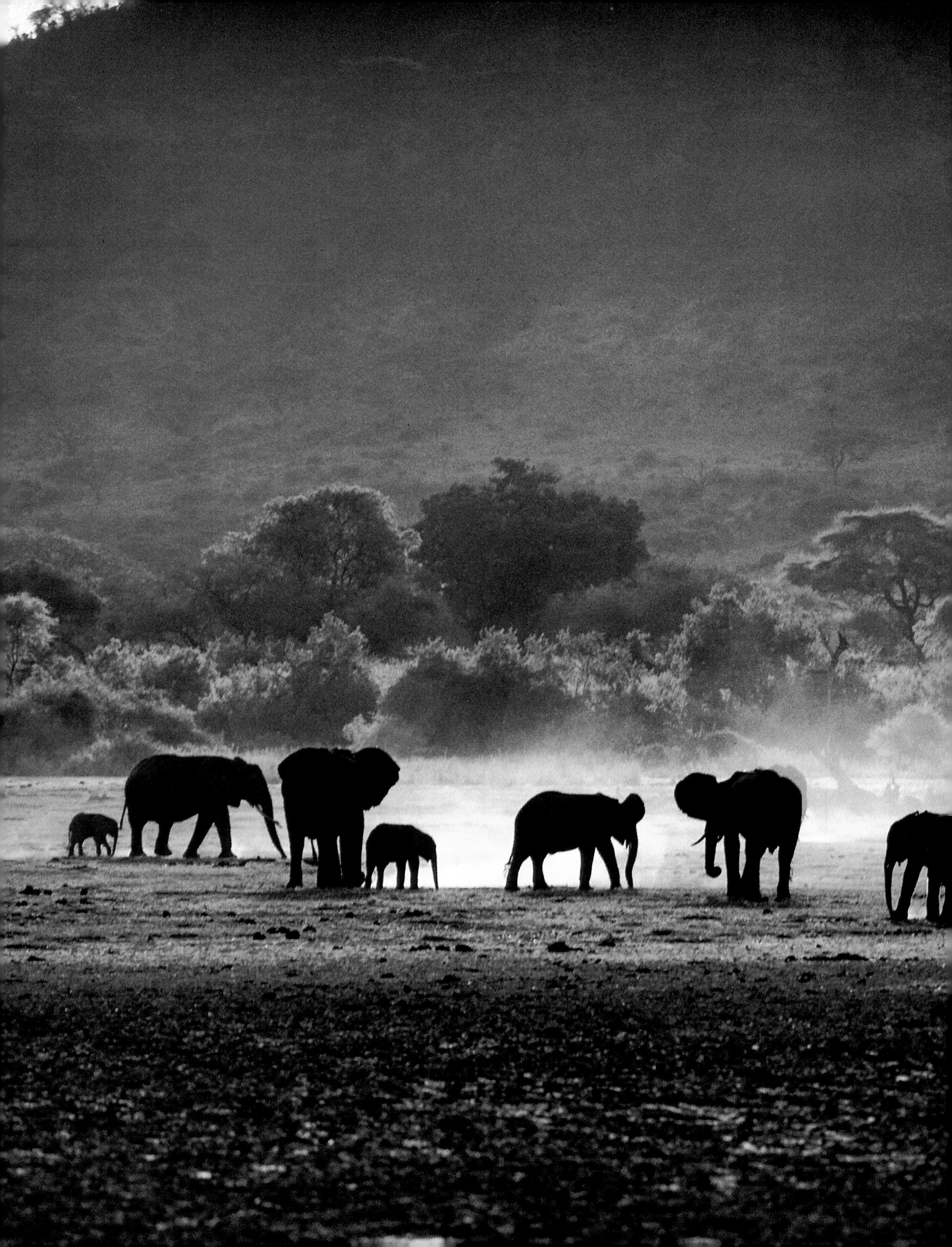

Stripping off the bark of an acacia feeds the elephant but kills the tree. Elephants can modify their environment like no other animal, with bulls able to extend their trunks up to 20 feet high into the canopy to crop the leaves. During the long dry season this may be the only source of green food and some have learned not only to pull down branches but to knock over whole trees. Given enough time these pachyderms can transform woodland into grassland. To supply their huge bodies with sufficient energy they have to feed for about eighteen hours a day. They keep moving long after the sun has gone down and only after midnight do they lie down for a few hours of sleep.

Before sunrise this bull (*opposite*) is already busy feeding. Elephants not only feed at night but also make use of those cool hours to walk to the water holes. In areas where the herds are under pressure from hunters and poachers they adopt a nocturnal life-style, emerging only after dark from their retreats in the dense thickets of the African bush. Next to feeding, dust- and mud-bathing are some of the elephants' favourite activities. Pasting their skin with mud not only cools it down but also serves to protect it from the harsh radiation of the sun.

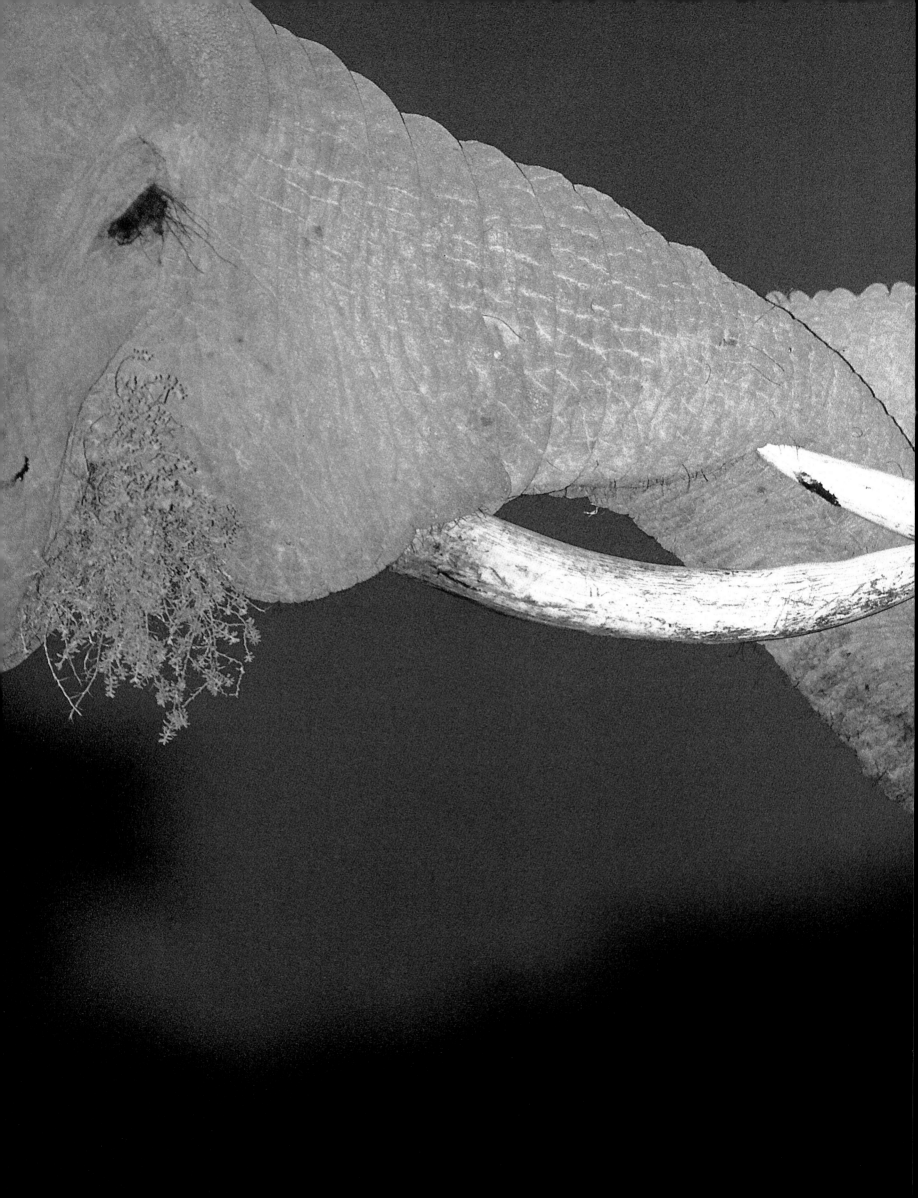

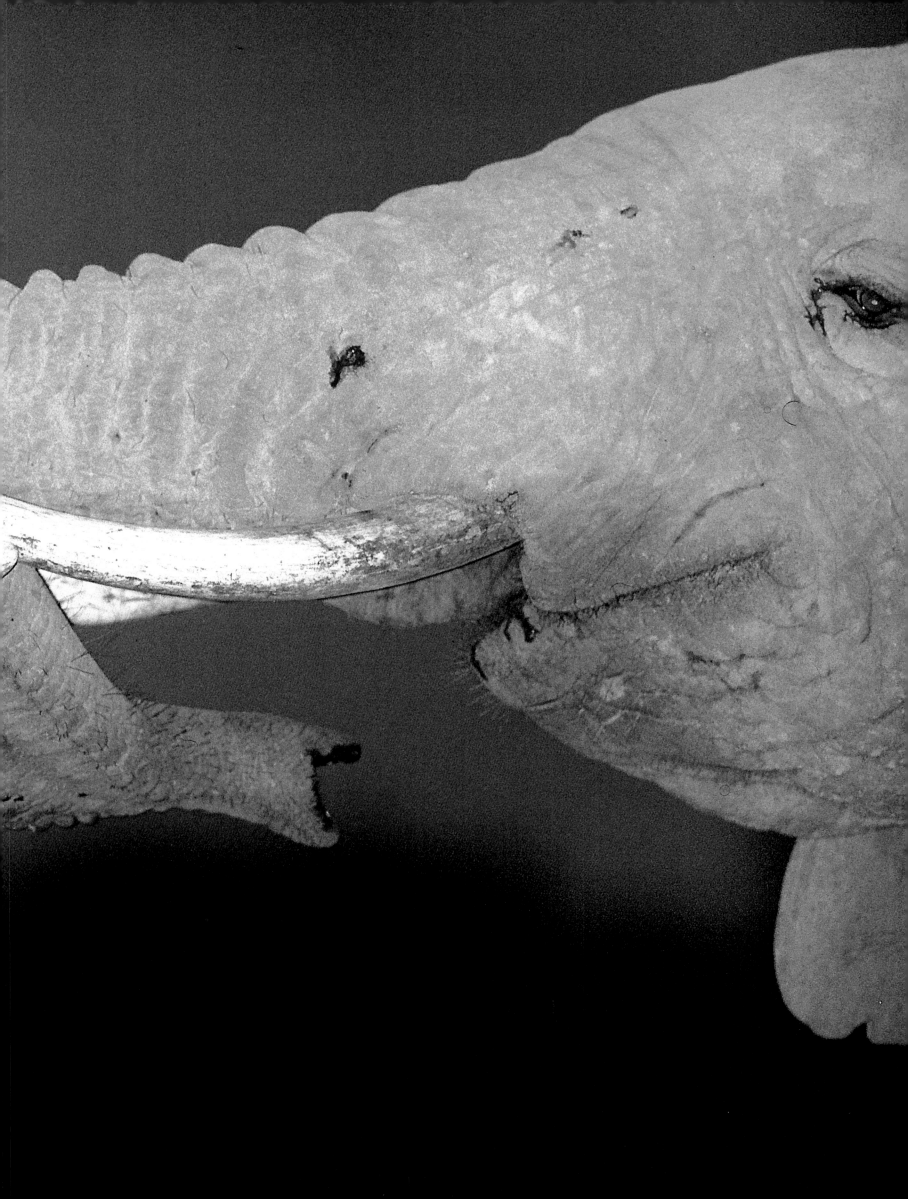

Once the coating has been applied it appears to be all the more fun to rub it off again. This bull (*opposite*) has found a branch to use as a brush — a tool that allows it to scratch itself in difficult places. Tool-use occurs very rarely amongst animals. Other well-known species which have incorporated the complex processes of tool-using into their behavioural patterns are chimps, sea-otters and Egyptian vultures. The skin of an elephant (*overleaf*) is convoluted with endless wrinkles, providing favoured sites for ticks and other such parasites to anchor themselves.

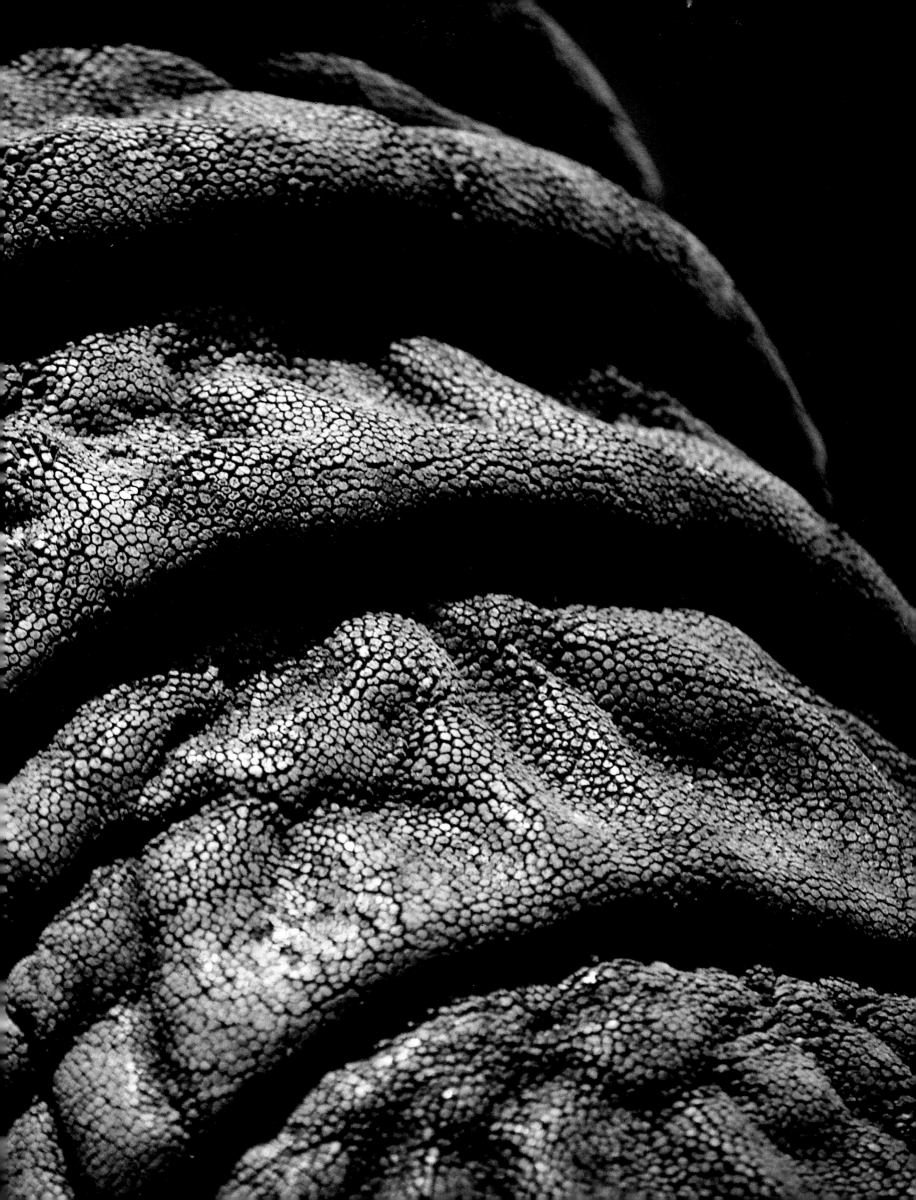

When bulls fight, trunks tie into knots and tusks clash. The sabre-rattling occurs quite frequently since the males start as juveniles to spar for their rank in the hierarchy. Only the highest-ranking bulls have a chance to mate with a female in œstrus and since this exciting event is a rare occurrence, the bulls at the top of the waiting list are rewarded by a high procreational premium. Tusks break off during these wrestling contests but serious or fatal injuries are rare. When one of the heavyweights has had enough, he simply moves away. Only when two bulls meet, both of which are in musth, will tusks lock into real battle, both fighters refusing to give an inch. Wisely, all other animals, including elephants, keep out of the way.

One rarely comes across mating elephants. Females come into œstrus only at long intervals and give birth to a calf every four to eight years. So most of the time when the bulls wander around the family units, they search in vain for any signs of a cow on heat. And even when a high-ranking bull does meet up with a female at just the right time, they only have a very quick affair. Mating can take less than a minute. But the excitement of the encounter spreads to all other members of the herd. They hurry in to greet the couple and mill around in an agitated, joyous way. Some even blow their trumpets as if in celebration of an elephant wedding.

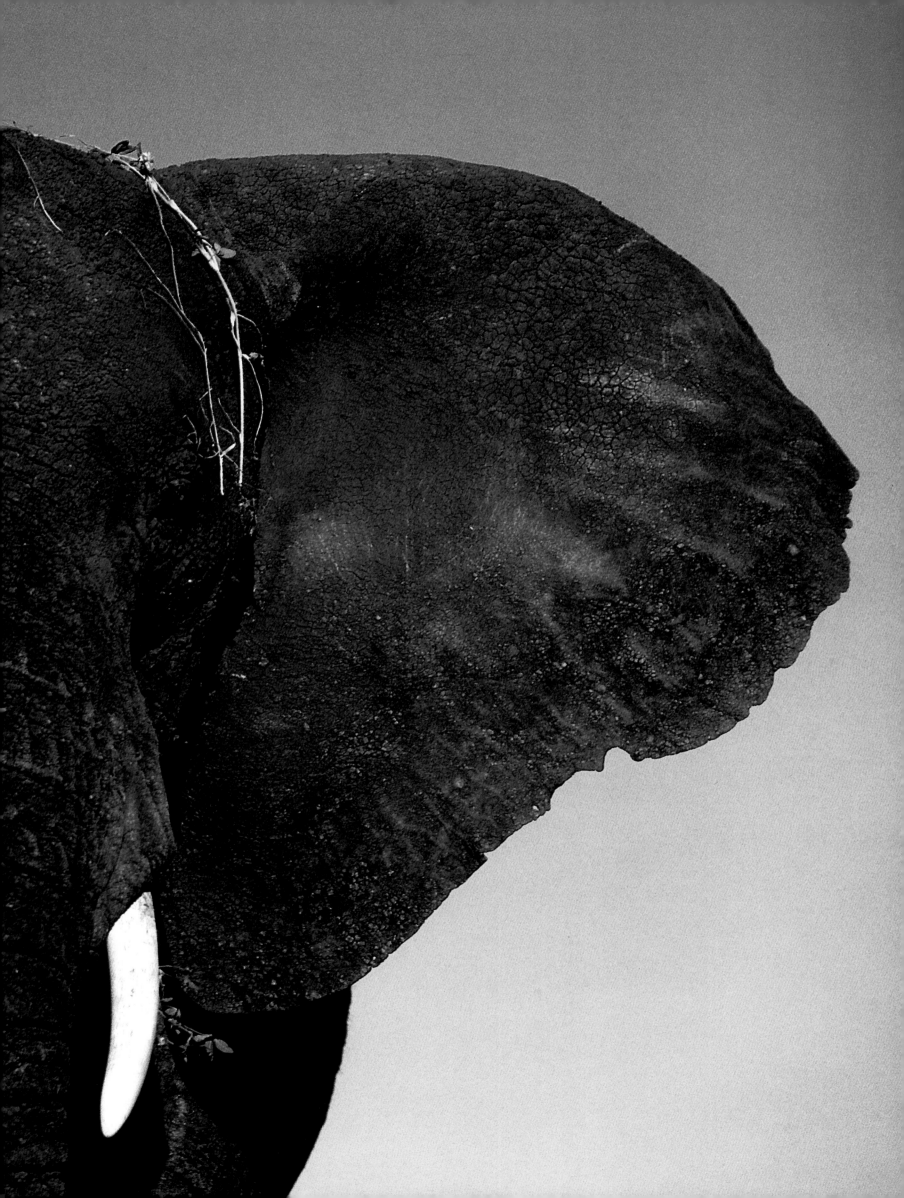

While feeding, herds usually split into small groups which then spread out in search of their huge daily requirements. But when they are on the move, the members of a herd tend to stick much closer together. Gliding over this herd (*overleaf*) near the woodlands in the western part of the Serengeti, I counted more than 130 elephants. At times the family units congregate into massive herds of 500 or more animals. Today one rarely comes across such an impressive gathering. Bulls sometimes like to wander off on their own. Occasionally they meet up with strangers, although elephants and rhinos generally avoid getting too close to one another. The tail of this black rhino betrays its discomfort in this situation.

of the calves, trunks can be a lifeline. Mothers calm their offspring by putting their trunks into the mouths of their young or by simply touching them. Even adults greet each other this way. In spite of their enormous size, elephants are highly sensitive. They act like gentle giants, at least most of the time, and when alarmed, need reassurance from one another. The trunk, packed with strong muscles and lined with very fine nerves, not only handles heavy tree trunks but also delicate crisis communications. For an elephant baby even a tail might help, although the safest place remains under the belly of their mother.

There are other havens too: between the mother's forelegs or squeezed in between mother and older sister. The calves, especially the small ones, need — and get — a lot of attention. Sometimes even more than they asked for. Concerned mothers help their calves across rocky stretches or push them up muddy banks. When the babies are born they already weigh about 220 pounds but are still so small that they have to stretch up high to reach their mothers' breasts. Red eyes are an indication that the nursing baby (*preceding pages*) is still at a very tender age.

lephants love water. Not only to drink and to shower themselves with but also to swim
n. They have been seen crossing deep rivers like the Nile or the Rufiji (*second spread
overleaf*) in southern Tanzania with just the tips of their trunks breaking the surface
This long natural snorkel provides the swimming heavyweights with all the breathing
air they need. Herds can cool off by splashing water over their backs and fresh greenery
such as reed-grass, grows close to the shores. Along the edges of Lake Manyara (*third
spread overleaf*) salty marsh grass, which elephants like for its taste, has attracted this
family unit.

One evening in the dry season I came across a small group of elephants drinking from a drying puddle of water. When the giants had quenched their thirst they plastered their bodies with the dark mud of the swamp. The light of the late afternoon gave the moisture on their skin the colour of dark bronze. I was transfixed by these primeval creatures whom the rays of the sun had cast into living sculptures. The elephant this lioness is feasting upon (*preceding pages*) has died of an illness.

Elephants seem to be most joyous and lively when they are near water. Not only do their bodies need more than 20 gallons of the precious liquid each day to keep their metabolisms going, but the pachyderms also seem to gain huge pleasure out of their daily walk to the water hole. It takes the babies about a year to master the art of using the trunk dangling out of their face as a hose-pipe. Until then, they must bend down to the surface to drink — a delicate task that requires a certain sense of balance without which there will most certainly be a splash.

The charge of an elephant is an impressive sight, even if it is only a single tusker that makes it. Their size and strength command respect from all other animals. One exception is a group of small bipedal creatures, which were already calling their bluff in the Stone Age. When those early hominids developed into Homo sapiens and pressed home their furious attacks with modern guns, the number of elephants began to dwindle. They are now nearly gone.

Tusks can be shaped in all sorts of ways. Sometimes the ivory teeth of females cross, which does not appear to inhibit their use of the trunk. Most of the time the tusks of big bulls curve outwards but this fine pair of evenly shaped weapons points inwards. One evening I went down to the shore of Lake Manyara (*overleaf*) to watch the moon rise. When I arrived, I realised that my view included a herd of elephants. Since I couldn't move them, I fixed them with my camera.